MURDER & MAYHEM
IN
METROWEST BOSTON

JAMES L. PARR AND KEVIN A. SWOPE

THE
History
PRESS

Published by The History Press
Charleston, SC
www.historypress.com

First published 2021

ISBN 9781540247544

Library of Congress Control Number: 2021931124

Notice: The information in this book is true and complete to the best of our knowledge. It is offered without guarantee on the part of the authors or The History Press. The authors and The History Press disclaim all liability in connection with the use of this book.

CONTENTS

ACKNOWLEDGEMENTS

The authors would like to thank the staff and volunteers at the Framingham History Center for all of their help in researching this book. We would also like to thank those who offered suggestions, including Andrea Haynes and Orlo Coots. Donna Russo at Historic New England was very helpful in helping us secure reproduction rights for the 1845 image of the Massachusetts Supreme Judicial Court justices. Special thanks are due to Georgina Hayward and Donna Peters for sharing their story and photos and to Ruthann Tomassini for connecting us to them.

INTRODUCTION

I f one excludes conflicts between European settlers and Native Americans, murder was remarkably uncommon in the cities and towns we now know as Boston's MetroWest before the second half of the nineteenth century. (Anyone who is interested in the region's colonial conflicts should consult the authors' previous book, *Framingham Legends and Lore*.) This is probably a function of a comparatively sparse population. For example, if one were to apply the state's 2019 murder rate (two per one hundred thousand population) historically, Massachusetts's annual death toll would not have reached ten until the 1820s. Considering there are currently 351 cities and towns in the state, that's not very many murders to go around. Even then, the murders were far from evenly distributed. Boston, as the largest and most urbanized community, had the lion's share of homicides. In the colonial period especially, most convictions and executions for murder were of women who had killed their newborn out-of-wedlock babies in an attempt to conceal a different crime of the time: fornication. Even so, most executions in New England in the 1600s and 1700s were for crimes other than homicide.

The most famous example of a non-homicide capital crime in the colonial era is, of course, witchcraft. The Salem Witch Hysteria of 1692 alone accounted for the hanging of nineteen individuals (fourteen women and five men), as well as another man, Giles Corey, who was pressed to death for refusing to enter a plea. (Oddly enough, two dogs were also executed.) Other capital crimes more common than homicide were piracy on the high seas, rape, arson and treason during the Revolutionary War. A number of Native Americans were executed during King Philip's War in 1676–77.

Even some property crimes were accorded the death penalty before 1800. Highwaymen, for example, were regularly executed. MetroWest, in fact, has the distinction of having been the scene of the crimes that led to the hanging of Samuel Smith, the last man to be executed for burglary in New England. Fifty-four-year-old Smith already had a significant criminal history in the summer of 1799, when he came to Sherborn, Massachusetts. A native of Middletown, Connecticut, he had been publicly whipped at Litchfield for stealing in the 1770s. He joined the Continental army for three years during the Revolution but deserted. After the war, he settled down as a farmer in Lancaster, Massachusetts, and started a family. He abandoned them in 1787, however, and pursued an itinerant life in New Hampshire. He was arrested later that year for stealing sheep in Concord, Massachusetts. Following his recapture after escaping from jail, he was pilloried and had his ears cut off. A few years later, he was back in prison, this time at Boston's Castle Island, for stealing silverware with the intent of using it to produce counterfeit coinage. In 1794, he was able to escape after twenty-eight months and headed to Pennsylvania. It was homesickness that brought him back to Sherborn five years later. On June 15, 1799, he broke into the home of Joseph Richards, stealing food and clothing. On June 20, he broke into another house in Natick. On June 22, he broke into Deacon William Tucker's storehouse in Sherborn. He cached the stolen articles in the woods in Sudbury, where a hunter came across them and notified the authorities. Smith was caught returning to retrieve his booty and was arrested. After a trial, he was found guilty of five counts of burglary in the first degree and hanged on the Common in Concord on the day after Christmas.

The earliest murder we were able to uncover in the region took place in Natick on November 2, 1693. Natick was then still a community of Native American Christian converts. A man named Jacob stabbed "Indian Tom" over an unknown dispute. Indian Tom died, and Jacob was brought to the Charlestown jail. He was tried and convicted, and according to David Allen Hearn's *Legal Executions in New England*, the source for much of the material in this chapter, Jacob "was almost certainly hanged on or about February 10, 1694."

What little we know about the murder of Indian Tom in 1693 comes from public records. With the rise of local newspapers in the 1800s, the coverage of crime, especially murder, became a staple of journalism and gave birth to the genre of true crime that is still popular today. The more information we have about both criminals and their victims enables us to recognize them as people not unlike ourselves. Human nature does not change, but societies do, and as writers, we hope these stories drawn from the history of our region demonstrate both qualities. This book is by no means a comprehensive account of all the murders in MetroWest. We have chosen some that we found intriguing for one reason or another, stories that we hope you agree are worth telling.

1

WAYLAND, 1838

A DOMESTIC TRAGEDY

The tragic events of the summer and fall of 1838 in the small village of Wayland, Massachusetts, will sadly sound familiar to the modern reader. It is a stark reminder that though we are tempted to romanticize the past, the ills that plague us now were also present then.

That view, namely that human nature is immutable and unchangeable, was not necessarily prevalent in 1830s Wayland. At the very least, it was a contested one. In the 1820s and 1830s, a wave of evangelical Protestant religious revivals, later termed the Second Great Awakening, swept through the northern United States. Contrary to today's image, the great social movements of the time generally found more adherents among the ranks of these "perfectionist" churches, who sought to improve both individuals and society as a whole through a zeal for reform. In this context, evangelical churches included not only Baptists and Methodists but also, in New England, Trinitarian Congregational churches, often formed from a schism with the more mainline Unitarian thought that had found favor among Boston's commercial elite and become prevalent at Harvard University. (The university was then still the leading source of clergymen for New England pulpits.) Out of this reform impulse came the antislavery movement, the temperance movement and the women's rights movement, all of which were intertwined.

Wayland in 1838 was a farming community of just under one thousand residents. Although it was the first part of Sudbury settled in 1638, by 1780, the majority of the town's land and population lived on the west side of the

Sudbury River. The residents of the east formed their own town, splitting off to become East Sudbury, renamed Wayland in 1835. Shortly after that, violence tore apart the Smith family.

Nathan Smith, a laborer, had married Anna Maynard on October 30, 1814. The couple lived in modest circumstances in Sudbury for the next twenty years and had at least seven children. About 1835 or so, Anna left her husband with the encouragement of her elder children. According to later accounts, Nathan Smith was an alcoholic who became physically abusive when he drank. Anna and the two youngest children moved to a house in Wayland, where she was supported by the earnings of her five older children, who lived and worked on farms in the area. Meanwhile, Nathan for a time had become a ward of the Town of Sudbury, probably living on the poor farm. (Divorce was exceedingly rare in those times and still carried with it a heavy stigma. It is unlikely that Anna had even considered that an option.)

By June 1838, Nathan Smith was employed again as a farmhand for Martin Moore. No doubt fortified by liquor, Smith walked to Wayland and burst through the door of his estranged wife's house. Anna, alarmed by the shouts of her husband, was able to gather her children and fled out the back door while Nathan broke through the front. Anna swore out a complaint against Nathan, but Wayland's town constable was unable to find him to serve the warrant. Throughout that summer, Nathan worked as a laborer, never staying in any one place very long.

At 10:00 p.m. on Thursday, September 27, 1838, after a bout of drinking, Nathan Smith again set out on foot from Sudbury to Wayland. Taking a roundabout route to evade being spotted and reported to the Wayland constable, he arrived at Anna's house at about 1:00 a.m. He was confident that he could overpower his wife, but he broke off a two-foot branch from a birch tree to use as a club should one of his older sons be at the house. From his experience in June, he knew the doors would be barred, so this time, he broke through a window in her bedchamber. Anna awoke and sprang to her feet immediately, but it was too late. Nathan dropped the branch and pinned her against the bed, pulling a jackknife from his pocket. She pleaded with him that she would return to live with him as his wife if he would spare her. But with two quick motions, it was over. His first jab with the knife had hit the back of her neck and struck mostly bone, but the second struck her jugular vein, ensuring she died almost instantaneously. Nathan went back out through the window and, once outside, cut his own throat and passed out. Regaining consciousness about dawn and shivering, he crawled back through the window into the house, lay down on the floor and covered himself in some of his wife's clothes and again passed out.

One of Anna's sons, who lived about a half mile away on the farm of Samuel Thompson, came to the house at about 1:00 p.m. the next afternoon. On seeing the smashed window, he went and looked inside. He saw his father motionless on the floor and his mother on the bed, with his five-year-old younger brother clinging to her lifeless body. He returned with help, and it was found that Nathan was still alive and expected to survive once his wound had been patched. Outside, the bloody jackknife was found at the spot where Nathan had attempted suicide.

When questioned, Nathan was unrepentant, saying, "My wife ought to be dead, she has treated me so bad." Her abandonment of him, her swearing out a complaint against him and the fact that his older children supported her and not him with their wages all fed his rage. Furthermore, one of the men for whom he had worked in Sudbury had refused to pay him for his labor and threatened to turn him in to the Wayland constable instead.

Later, when Nathan Smith was being transported to the jail in Concord, the wagon passed through Sudbury and past his wife's family's house, where she was laid out on a bed, waiting to be buried. He and Anna had been married there nearly twenty-four years earlier. Nathan remarked to one of his captors, "I have returned her to the house from which I took her, and if I had done within a year after we were married, it would have been better for me."

In 1838, all capital cases were heard by the Massachusetts Supreme Judicial Court, and in those days, the court still traveled a circuit throughout the counties of the commonwealth. This caused Nathan Smith to languish in jail for a long time (by nineteenth-century standards) before going to trial. He was not arraigned until seven months later, in April 1839, and his trial before the justices, Lemuel Shaw, Marcus Morton and Samuel Sumner Wilde, did not begin until Monday, June 3, when the court next sat in Lowell. He pled not guilty, although the evidence he had committed the act was overwhelming. G.F. Farley and A.H. Nelson, his attorneys, instead had argued diminished capacity through insanity, but the jury returned a guilty verdict shortly after the court recessed at 6:00 p.m. on Wednesday, June 5.

The sentencing took place on Friday morning, with Chief Justice Lemuel Shaw pronouncing Nathan Smith's fate. At the age of fifty-eight, the crusty Federalist was nine years into what would prove to be an extremely influential thirty-year career as the commonwealth's senior jurist. Shaw's rulings and written opinions reshaped common law to accommodate an

Lemuel Shaw (1781–1861) served as chief justice of the Massachusetts Supreme Judicial Court for thirty years. *Courtesy of Library of Congress.*

increasingly industrialized society, not only for Massachusetts but also for the United States as a whole. After reflecting on the evidence and fairness of the trial, Shaw proceeded to address the nature of the crime itself. The words of the revered justice were so stirring that they were widely reproduced in newspapers throughout New England. "If there be any crime, at which humanity shudders and starts back with affright, it is murder," Shaw intoned and then continued:

> *And who was the victim of your malicious violence? A stranger, an enemy? Or even a fellow citizen, entitled to the protection of the same laws as yourself, and to whom life was as dear as to yourself? She was indeed this and much more. She was the wife of your youth, the companion of your youth, the companion of your better days, the mother of your children; not only one whose rights you were bound to respect, but on whom you had solemnly pledged yourself to protect, to cherish, and to love. She may have had faults—she may have done you wrong—you might have just cause of complaint—whether you had or not, we know not and ask not; you had no right to take vengeance into your own hands. Every consideration of manly feeling, of social duty, of moral and religious obligation, ought to have restrained your hand and your heart, from the execution of the cruel deed. Yet regardless of these considerations, you stole upon her solitary dwelling,*

at the dead of night, violently burst into her humble room, her and your unhappy child sleeping at her side, and notwithstanding her agonizing cry to you to spare her life, you plunged the knife into her throat, and violently deprived her of existence.

Shaw then turned to what he saw as the root of Smith's evil deed.

There is one circumstance which stands out conspicuously among the facts appearing on a review of your unhappy case, to which I feel bound on present occasion to allude. It appears by the whole tenor of the evidence, that for many years you have been in the habit of indulging in the intemperate use of ardent spirits, and for several years to an increasing and mischievous extent....Until you had permitted yourself to indulge in this intemperate excess, nothing appears to show that you were not amiable, respected and happy, a hardworking and industrious man, with a beloved family and a happy home. But after you had become addicted to the habitual use of intoxicating liquors, all this was sadly reversed; you were occasionally visited by delirium and sickness; you became separated from your wife; your children were scattered; your home was abandoned, and you became a pauper and an outcast....May we not indulge the hope, that your example, trying and painful as it is, may stand forth as a prominent beacon light warning all, and more especially the young, to avoid the first approach to the use of ardent spirits, seeing how direct tendency it has to lead to habitual intemperance, and through intemperance, to the most atrocious crimes... showing incontrovertibly, that intemperance is the prolific mother of misery, vice, and crime.

Shaw instructed the prisoner to repent and prepare his soul for the end. He then concluded his speech with these words: "And now it only remains to pronounce the solemn sentence, which the law affixes to the crime of which you stand convicted, which is that you, Nathan Smith, be taken back to the prison from whence you came, and thence at such time as the Executive Government of the Commonwealth may, by their warrant, appoint, to the place of execution, and there be hung by the neck, until you are dead. And may God, of his abundant and inexhaustible goodness, have mercy on your soul."

In the end, Nathan Smith succeeded in cheating the hangman. Four days later, on June 11, 1839, he was found hanging in his cell at Lowell by his pocket handkerchief and a small cord.

2

STOW, 1844

THE MOWING MURDER

A t ten o'clock in the evening of September 2, 1844, a wagon clattered through the darkness of the sleepy village of Stow, Massachusetts. Two men were riding home, relying on their horse to find its way along the Hudson road on that cloudy, dimly lit Monday night. They had almost reached the junction where one would either turn left toward Marlborough or right toward Sudbury, when their horse suddenly took fright, and the wagon jerked to a stop. Unable to make out the trouble from where they sat, the men jumped down onto the road, seeking to calm the animal and discover what had spooked it so. There, just ahead of the horse in a ditch along the side of the road, lay the motionless body of a man. At first glance, they could tell he was a sizable, powerfully built man. His skin was cold to the touch; he was obviously dead and likely had been for hours. They scrambled to fetch a lantern from the wagon. In the flickering light, the cause of death became evident—his head had nearly been detached from his neck, clearly the work of an axe. They recognized him as George Washington Hildreth, an athletic man in his early thirties who lived just across the town line in neighboring Bolton.

In the morning, Stow's selectmen gathered to investigate. The body had been found practically on the doorstep of the Goldsmith house, so it made sense to begin inquiries there. The selectmen found thirty-six-year-old Eunice (Rice) Goldsmith at home with her seven children, but her husband, fifty-one-year-old William, was nowhere to be found. Eunice reported that she had last seen William shortly after dusk the evening before. He had burst through the door demanding "his best hat and coat" and announced he must be off at once. He had yet either to return or send word of his whereabouts. The selectmen immediately offered the impressive sum of $100 for his apprehension, which they soon doubled to $200. Early speculation in the *Newburyport Herald* had him "supposed to go to New-York." A week passed, then two, but there was still no sign of the fugitive William Goldsmith.

When he was spotted exactly three weeks following the murder, on September 23, 1844, it was in the opposite direction of New York. A traveling peddler in Wilton, New Hampshire, recognized Goldsmith from the handbill that had been issued by the Stow selectmen and took him into custody. (Wilton had not been chosen at random. The murder suspect's uncle and namesake, William Goldsmith, had settled in the town in the 1770s, and he still had relatives living there.) His time in hiding had worn on him, however, and he gave himself up freely. The *Concord Freeman* described his countenance as that of a "helpless child," his appearance contrasting sharply with the brutality of the act of which he was accused. The peddler delivered his quarry back across the Massachusetts border to Stow, where he collected his bounty. After an examination, Goldsmith was remanded to the jail in Concord. Soon reports were circulating that Goldsmith was a sympathetic figure, and perhaps murder charges would not even be brought against him.

The decision of whether to prosecute would not be made by the anonymous scribes of the local newspapers, however; it would be made by the district attorney for the counties of Essex and Middlesex, Asahel Huntington. An attorney in Salem, Huntington had been educated at Phillips Andover and graduated from Yale in the class of 1819. Although only forty-six years old, he had already served as the chief prosecutor in two counties for nearly fifteen years. The Hildreth murder case coincided with the nadir of his career. Earlier in 1844, Huntington had been accused of embezzling funds entrusted to his care. The charges were investigated by the judiciary committee of the Massachusetts legislature. After a six-month investigation, the committee issued its report in January 1845, clearing Huntington of the charges. The episode had greatly depressed him and broken his health, and it was several months before he resumed his duties. Meanwhile, William Goldsmith's own health could not have been aided by a winter spent in the jail at Concord. Finally, in April 1845, seven months after his arrest, William Goldsmith was arraigned at Lowell for the murder of George Washington Hildreth.

The law office of Edward Mellen (1802–1875), who defended William Goldsmith, still stands on the Common in Wayland Center. *Photo by author.*

Goldsmith's defense was handled by attorneys Edward Mellen and Charles Smith of Wayland. Mellen had graduated from Brown University and was close friends with its president, Reverend Francis Wayland. (In 1835, Mellen had been the one who prevailed upon his fellow residents of East Sudbury to rename itself in Wayland's honor. In turn, the university president had helped to endow the town's library.) Mellen operated his practice from a small office located on the town's Common, where the two-room white clapboard structure still stands to this day. Smith appears to have been Mellen's junior partner and less prominent in town affairs.

The trial was held the first week of June 1845, when the Supreme Judicial Court made its annual visit to Lowell. Chief Justice Lemuel Shaw presided, as he had over the trial of Nathan Smith six years earlier, once again assisted by associate justice Samuel Sumner Wilde. In the interim, Marcus Morton had retired from the court to serve as governor, so the third justice on the panel was relative newcomer Samuel Hubbard. All three were Yankees of the old school, both figuratively and literally—they graduated from Harvard, Dartmouth and Yale, respectively. Wilde was seventy-four years old, Shaw sixty-four and Hubbard the youngest at fifty-nine.

Justices Samuel Hubbard (1785–1847), Samuel Sumner Wilde (1771–1855) and Lemuel Shaw (1781–1861) of the Massachusetts Supreme Judicial Court, circa 1845. *Courtesy of Historic New England.*

Prosecutor Huntington's case was straightforward: Goldsmith had confessed to killing Hildreth. That George Washington Hildreth had walked down the road and encountered William Goldsmith in his yard, the two had argued and Goldsmith had struck him down with a mortal blow of an axe was uncontested. Goldsmith's attorneys, while not challenging that narrative, sought to provide context for the encounter. Goldsmith, a man of modest means, was a hardworking family man. He had served the nation in the War of 1812 from his native Andover. A number of Stow neighbors testified that his character was "as good as that of people in general."

By contrast, Hildreth was described as "quarrelsome" and "intemperate," which in those days meant he drank, and two partially consumed bottles of rum were found in the pockets of his coat. As we learned in the case of Nathan Smith, Chief Justice Shaw was ardently against intoxicating spirits. If anything, Samuel Hubbard was even more so; Hubbard had been a cofounder and president of the American Society for the Promotion of Temperance. Goldsmith's attorneys had reason to feel optimistic for their client's chances of avoiding the hangman.

William Goldsmith and George Washington Hildreth had a long-standing quarrel over grass mowing. The precise nature of the dispute has been lost to time, but hay for livestock was not a trivial concern to farmers. Neighbors testified that Hildreth had often threatened "to whip Goldsmith, ride him on a wall, spoil his head, and other like expressions," while Goldsmith had generally sought to avoid encountering Hildreth at all. On that fateful September 2, Goldsmith had bought a leg of beef from a neighbor and was using an axe to cut it up in the yard in front of his house. According to Goldsmith, a drunken Hildreth had seen him from the road and proceeded to taunt him until matters escalated and Hildreth came after him. As Hildreth was twenty years younger and a much stronger man, Goldsmith had swung the axe in his defense, not knowing which way he had the blade or blunt end facing. Hildreth fell to the ground without uttering another word. Panicking, Goldsmith then fled. Clearly, Mellen and Smith argued, this was a case of self-defense and warranted an acquittal.

The jury retired at 1:30 p.m. on Wednesday, June 4, 1845, and deliberated for three and a half hours. At 5:00 p.m., they returned with their verdict. The jurors found Goldsmith guilty, but of manslaughter, not murder. The justices imposed what was for the era the relatively light sentence of three days solitary confinement and seven years of hard labor at the state prison. According to a later town history, Goldsmith was pardoned before serving his full sentence. We know that he served at least five years, because he was recorded as an inmate serving time for manslaughter at the Charlestown State Prison when the U.S. Census was taken on September 13, 1850. Following his release, Goldsmith returned to Stow, where he lived out his

This image from the 1850 U.S. Census lists inmates at the Massachusetts State Prison in Charlestown and their offenses. William Goldsmith is on the bottom line with his crime, "Man Slaughter." *Courtesy of the National Archives and Records Administration.*

days quietly, collecting a pension for his service in the War of 1812, until he died there on April 30, 1869, at the age of seventy-six. His widow, Eunice, lived another twenty-five years, dying in Stow in 1894.

As for the two young boys of the man Goldsmith killed, Joseph Oscar Hildreth (aged two years) and Horatio Nelson Hildreth (newborn) went to live with cousins in Berlin, where they learned the shoemaker's trade. Each served in the Civil War and survived. Horatio died in an Old Soldier's Home in Illinois in 1918, while Joseph died in Worcester, Massachusetts, three years later. Their mother never remarried. She lived with her parents in Bolton and died in Hudson in 1881.

3

SOUTH NATICK, 1852

THE CORDWAINER'S APPRENTICE

E arly on the morning of September 18, 1852, Isaac Hall was startled to find six-year-old Ouvra Taylor Jr. and his five-year-old sister, Agnes, standing in the front hall of his home in South Natick, both still in their bedclothes. "Our parents were killed—we want to stop and live here," explained the boy. It was quarter past six on a Saturday morning, barely a half hour past sunrise, and Hall struggled to make sense of the scene before him. "Are they still in bed?" he asked, wondering if perhaps they were ill. The boy seemed to indicate that they were. "Why don't you take me to them?" Hall asked. At that, young Ouvra immediately recoiled and began trembling.

Leaving the children with his sister-in-law, Isaac Hall and his younger brother, Alfred, set out across the road to find out what was happening at the Taylor house. Ouvra Taylor Sr. was a thirty-year-old cordwainer who had moved to Natick in the 1840s from rural Vienna, Maine. (In the old parlance, a cordwainer made brand-new shoes from fresh leather, as distinguished from a cobbler, who merely repaired shoes.) Taylor had married Angelina Davis, the daughter of a farmer in neighboring Sherborn, and they settled in to raise a family in the Natick neighborhood known as the Little South Village. The small one-and-a-half-story house stood on the south side of Everett Street just east of the Cottage Street intersection. There were three rooms on the first floor: kitchen, bedchamber and front room, with a small ell attached to the back that contained Ouvra's shoemaking shop. Upstairs under the eaves were two small sleeping chambers. The three older Taylor

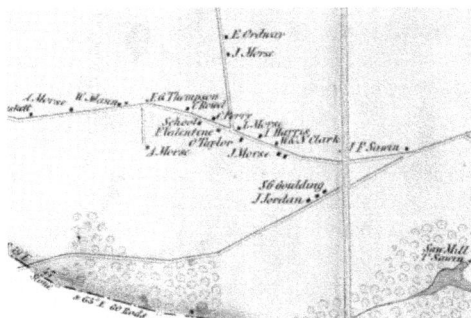

Detail from the 1853 map of Natick depicting the Little South Natick neighborhood. Ouvra Taylor's house is labeled "O. Taylor" and Isaac Hall's labeled "I. Harris" after its previous resident. *Courtesy of Framingham History Center.*

children shared one, while the other had been occupied for the previous six weeks by Thomas Casey, the shoemaker's nineteen-year-old apprentice. In exchange for six months' labor, Casey was to receive room and board and thirty dollars.

Casey was fresh off the boat from Ireland and had only been with Taylor since early August. He was probably the same Thomas Casey, aged twenty, who had arrived in Boston from Limerick, Ireland, aboard the brig *Charles* of Galway on June 21, 1852. Casey had a first cousin, James Casey, who lived in Natick and came from Kilfenora in County Clare. Thomas was likely from the same small village in the west of Ireland, about equidistant from the ports of Galway and Limerick. It probably was not a coincidence that he was hired by Ouvra Taylor so soon after arriving in the United States. Taylor was known as sober and hardworking, but the shoemaker's trade was not a prosperous one in 1850s Massachusetts. At least one former apprentice, Scotsman Duncan Matheson, had been spreading word around Natick that Ouvra Taylor did not pay fairly and in fact still owed him money for work he had done a year before. Taylor's most recent apprentice had lasted but a short time before leaving. A young immigrant unfamiliar with Taylor's reputation might have been the only person willing to sign on as his apprentice.

As the Hall brothers approached the Taylor house, they instinctively went around back. Isaac and Alfred had been to the Taylors' countless times since they had moved to the neighborhood the previous December, always entering via the shop. They found the door had been left ajar. Stepping inside, they saw Ouvra Taylor lying motionless on his right side on the shop floor, his stool overturned behind him. His feet were near his workbench, and his head was near the hallway door. He had several wounds on the back of his head and neck. Each proved severe enough to have been fatal, but one had been administered with such force that it had nearly decapitated the shoemaker. An axe, still covered in blood, had been left leaning against the doorjamb.

Entering the main part of the house, the brothers saw the bedroom door open, but the bed was empty. Farther down the short hallway, the door to the front room was wide open. Gazing in, they were confronted with a vision of unimaginable horror. There, in the center of the room, lay Angeline Taylor in her nightclothes surrounded by a pool of clotted blood. Her head rested on the seat of a small nursing rocking chair. A single enormous gash cleaved her forehead down to her left eyebrow, deep enough that brain tissue could be seen in the wound. Next to her on the floor slept her youngest child, eighteen-month-old toddler Ella Taylor. All around them, the walls of the room were splattered with dried blood. Isaac Hall was stunned to discover that Angeline was still breathing and opened her eyes when he asked her the somewhat incongruous question, "What is the matter?" Leaving Mrs. Taylor, Isaac ran to fetch help from his neighbors while Alfred took Ella across the road to be cared for by his wife and then returned for the fourth Taylor child, incredibly still asleep upstairs. There was no sign of Thomas Casey. The alarm was raised, and riders were sent in all directions to locate the missing apprentice.

At about 8:00 a.m., forty-one-year-old Framingham straw merchant Alexander Clark was riding in his carriage on the road from Sherborn when he passed a young man in a Kossuth hat walking hurriedly in the same direction. Arriving at the South Framingham train depot, Clark quickly learned of the horrible murder that had taken place in Natick. When the constable gave a description of the missing apprentice, Clark immediately thought of the man he had passed on the road and offered to drive the constable to find him. They went back down the Sherborn road (today's Beaver Street/Kendall Avenue), but there was no sign of the man. Heading back to the depot, Clark this time drove his horse south onto the Holliston Road (Hollis Street). There, at about 8:30 a.m., he spotted the man again; he must have cut through the fields and woods, as there was no road but the one they had ridden on. Clark pulled the carriage up alongside.

"Where are you traveling from?" inquired Clark.

"The railroad in Natick," Casey replied.

"That's impossible; I just passed you not a half hour ago heading up the road from Sherborn."

At that, Casey admitted he had come from South Natick, where he worked for Ouvra Taylor. He had left between eight and ten o'clock the night before; there was no clock in the house, so he could not be sure. He spent the night in Needham (probably in the section that was later set off as Wellesley) and "straying about in the woods." Mr. Taylor knew he had gone, and he left the house at night to save time. When asked where he was headed, Casey replied to see his brother in Worcester. "Well then you're heading in the wrong direction!" Clark said. "Get in and I'll take you to the Framingham depot." There they spread the word that Casey had been found and dropped the pretense of giving the Irishman a ride. Inspecting Casey's clothing, they found no obvious traces of blood. Casey had only four cents in his possession. Then they

Alexander Clark (1811–1890), a Framingham straw bonnet manufacturer, found Thomas Casey wandering the roads and assisted the constable in his apprehension. *Courtesy of Framingham History Center.*

brought Casey back to the scene of the murder. The apprentice appeared impassive on viewing the lifeless body of his master and his grievously wounded mistress. From there, he was brought to Natick Town Hall, where Justice Chester Adams remanded the prisoner to the Concord jail until his arraignment on Monday morning.

Casey was not the only suspect in custody, however. Duncan Matheson, Taylor's former apprentice, had been pulled off a Pictou-bound schooner on the Boston waterfront. Matheson was well-known for his grievances against Taylor and had been heard to remark that the shoemaker "must expect to suffer if he does not pay his debts." Matheson's employer confirmed his alibi for Friday night, and it appears his imminent departure for Nova Scotia had been a coincidence. After a few days, Matheson was sent on his way.

Coroner Alexander Coolidge called an inquest into the death of Ouvra Taylor. The jury convened at the Taylor house to inspect the scene. It was one of the jurors, Samuel H. Colbath, who found the apprentice's apron on the floor in the shop and noted what looked like blood on the strap used to fasten the garment. The men formally concluded that Taylor had died from wounds administered by his apprentice, Thomas Casey.

Meanwhile, Angeline Taylor lay prostrate in bed under the care of thirty-five-year-old Dr. John Hoyt, who gave no hope for her recovery. She was intermittently conscious but evidently unable to speak. Her two oldest children were brought to her bedside. When she reached out to her son, Ouvra, he immediately drew back in fear, and the children were taken away again. The young doctor asked her several times who had killed her husband. Although she attempted to answer, her words were unintelligible. "If Casey killed your husband, squeeze my hand." She pressed his hand for about thirty seconds.

Saturday evening brought a visit from Dr. Simon Whitney of Framingham Centre. Twenty years Hoyt's senior, Dr. Whitney was the region's most respected physician. Grasping Angeline's hand in his, he asked, "If the Irishman, Casey, was the murderer of your husband, will you squeeze my hand?" Again, the response was a weak but discernible tightening of her grip on Whitney's fingers.

By Sunday, news of the attack had spread throughout the area. After church services let out that day, throngs of friends, neighbors and the simply curious converged on Little South Village to inspect the scene of the crime firsthand. By nightfall, literally hundreds of people had filed through the Taylor house.

The next morning, another crowd packed into the Natick Town Hall to witness the arraignment of Thomas Casey. The correspondent from the *Boston Herald* described him as a "young, lusty Irishman, having nothing remarkable about him." He had "one of those faces that would never be noticed in a crowd." The journalist went on to dispel one of the rumors that had spread over the weekend, remarking that "to say that he is of a very low order of intellect is mere nonsense."

The presiding officer was Natick's sixty-seven-year-old justice of the peace, Chester Adams. He had held most every office his fellow townsmen could award him: twenty-seven years as town secretary and treasurer, five terms as state representative and two as state senator. He had been postmaster at South Natick for seven years, until the Van Buren administration replaced the old-line-Federalist-turned-Whig Adams with a Democrat. On this occasion, Adams was assisted by two justices from neighboring Framingham, Joseph Fuller and Lorenzo Sabine.

Representing the state was attorney John W. Bacon of Natick, Harvard class of 1843, filling in for Middlesex district attorney Charles R. Train, otherwise detained. Casey was represented by Constantine Canaris Esty of Framingham, Yale class of 1845, assisted by C.C. Andrew of Newton. A parade of witnesses, beginning with the Hall brothers, laid out the facts of the case. Through it all, Casey remained silent, declining to testify on his own behalf. In rebuttal, Esty observed that there was no physical evidence tying Casey to the crime. Nor, for that matter, had any witnesses suggested any discord between apprentice and master, never mind a motive for murder. Adams remained unconvinced. Casey had been the last known person to see the shoemaker alive, the justice reasoned, and when found wandering in the woods in Framingham the next morning, he could give no coherent reason why he had left the Taylor house that night. Hearing that he was to remain jailed until trial, the apprentice visibly lost his composure for the first time since he had been accosted on the Holliston Road two days earlier. The *Boston Herald*'s reporter thought Casey appeared "surly" as he struggled with the constables trying to place him in handcuffs for the ride back to Concord.

Angeline Taylor died at 4:00 p.m. that same afternoon, Monday, September 21, 1852. The funeral, planned for the next day, would now be for both husband and wife. Mourners gathered at 2:00 p.m. at the First Congregational Church in Natick Center. Reverend W.H. Watson, Baptist minister, gave out a hymn, and the Reverend Edmund Dowse of Sherborn offered a closing prayer. The funeral oration was delivered by the church's pastor, Reverend Elias Nason. Speaking of the orphaned Taylor brood, Nason thundered, "Who shall answer to their innocent call for 'father,' or for 'mother,'

Chester Adams (1785–1858) served Natick as town clerk, state representative, state senator and colonel of the militia. As justice of the peace, he presided over the arraignment of Thomas Casey. *Courtesy of Framingham History Center.*

Constantine Canaris Esty (1824–1912) was a prominent Framingham attorney who represented Thomas Casey at his arraignment. He later served the town as a state representative, state senator and, briefly, congressman. *Courtesy of Framingham History Center.*

and for 'bread'?" Answering his own question, he continued, "Can the cold grave reply to thee? Oh no! But thanks unto God there is one who heareth the young ravens when they cry, who marks the sparrow's fall, and 'tempers the wind to the shorn lamb.' He will provide for them, and we beseech of thee, O Christ, that thou wilt be a father and a mother and an Almighty Savior to them!"

At the conclusion of the emotional service, a collection was taken up for the children. The generosity of their neighbors ensured that each of the three children who survived to adulthood received in excess of $200 on his or her twenty-first birthday, in addition to whatever expenses the fund had covered in childhood. By contrast, Ouvra and Angeline's entire estate amounted to $92.45, and that was prior to any expenses being deducted.

Reverend Elias Nason (1811–1887), Congregational clergyman and author, delivered a powerful eulogy for the slain Ouvra and Angeline Taylor. *Courtesy of Framingham History Center.*

After the funeral, the coffins were taken outside and placed on a stand on the Town Common. The lids were removed, and congregants filed past for a final look at the deceased. According to a newspaper report, "Mrs. Taylor, from her long suffering, looked ghastly; but the countenance of Mr. Taylor was fresh, and nothing but the partial view of the wounds betokened a violent death." After a time, the lids were replaced, the coffins loaded on a wagon and a long procession of carriages set off on the two-mile journey to the Plain Burial Ground in Sherborn. There, Ouvra and Angeline were laid to rest in the Davis family plot.

A few weeks later, on October 10, Joseph Critcherson of Natick was walking through the woods in South Framingham when he discovered a shirt folded up and tucked "in a sort of hollow under the roots of tree." It had stains on it, which he thought could well have been blood. He immediately thought of Thomas Casey's wanderings on the night of September 17–18 and turned it over to authorities.

Thomas Casey was moved to Lowell in October, when he was formally indicted, and he remained there through April 1853, when he was arraigned. The trial itself was held off until May, when the court next convened in East Cambridge, the seat of the Southern Middlesex District.

In February 1853, Casey welcomed two unusual visitors to his cell in the Lowell jail. Ann Green and Mary Jane Eastman were both "factory girls" in Lowell. They had had no previous contact with Thomas Casey. Though their reason for visiting the jail was never stated, it seems likely that the authorities had recruited the young women as potentially sympathetic listeners to elicit a confession from the prisoner. Ann Green went first. Standing outside the bars, she looked in to see Casey sitting on his bunk holding a book upside down. She asked if he was able to read. "A little," was his reply. She asked if he felt bad, and he said yes. Dispensing with small talk, she got down to business: "Are you the murderer of Mr. and Mrs. Taylor?" He said he was. At this point, she asked the jailer to admit her into his cell. Mary Jane Eastman accompanied her. According to their later testimony, he was unable to state why he had done it but admitted he had used an axe and that the bloody shirt found in the woods was probably his.

The trial of Thomas Casey finally commenced on Monday, May 16, 1853. The presiding officer was, once again, Lemuel Shaw, then in his twenty-third year as chief justice of the Massachusetts Supreme Judicial Court. In the Casey trial, Shaw was assisted by associate justices Theron Metcalf and Pliny Merrick. The government's case was presented by the ambitious Middlesex district attorney Charles Russell Train. Thirty-six-year-old Train had been born in Framingham, the son of the town's Baptist minister. He was a graduate of Brown University and had attended Harvard Law School and would later serve in Congress and as Massachusetts attorney general. Train was aided by Massachusetts attorney general Rufus Choate, the former Whig congressman and senator.

Casey had some legal firepower of his own. G.A. Somerby was a respected Newton attorney, but the lead defense counsel was the indomitable (and always controversial) Benjamin Franklin Butler of Lowell. An 1838 graduate of Waterville (now Colby) College, Butler had made a name for himself as a pugnacious trial lawyer, always ready to pounce on any errors made by the prosecution. He was also famous as a Democratic politician and champion of the ten-hour workday. Although his greatest successes and controversies lay ahead of him, he

Charles R. Train (1817–1885) was the Middlesex County district attorney who prosecuted the case against Thomas Casey. *Courtesy of Framingham History Center.*

was already anathema to the state's establishment embodied by Chief Justice Shaw and Attorney General Choate. (One of the more unusual items in the collection of the Massachusetts Historical Society is a porcelain chamber pot with a portrait of Benjamin Butler at the bottom of the bowl, no doubt donated by a blue-blooded Beacon Hill family.)

The trial itself was comparatively straightforward. District Attorney Train methodically laid out the government's case. According to the prosecution, Casey and Taylor had stayed up working in the shop after the rest of the household had retired to bed. They had an argument—a thirteen-year-old neighbor, George D. Perry, testified that he had heard them shouting at each other—and Casey had repeatedly struck Ouvra Taylor from behind with an axe. The nature of the argument was never made clear, although it might have been about the quality of the apprentice's work; the prosecution produced a poorly pegged shoe found on the floor of the shop. Angeline Taylor had come into the shop and then retreated into the bedroom where Casey swung the axe at her and missed, splitting off a large chunk of the bedpost, which was shown to the jury. She then fled into the parlor, where she succeeded in shutting the door on her assailant. Casey used the axe to pry open the door, as indicated by marks on the doorjamb, and then struck Angeline once with the axe and left her for dead. He ran upstairs to change his bloody shirt—there was a trail of blood spots leading up the stairs and into his sleeping chamber—and then fled out the back door of the shop, heading east toward Needham, as evidenced by Casey's own statements the next morning and a series of footprints in the Taylor garden that ended at the neighbor's cornfield. The next morning, he was seen zigzagging through fields and woods until he was picked up by Alexander Clark's carriage.

Other than pointing out that parts of the government's case were pure conjecture, Benjamin Butler only challenged one point: the dying declaration of Mrs. Taylor. Butler suggested that her squeezing of the doctors' hands when asked if Casey had been the murderer could not be considered a "dying declaration" as it was understood under the common law, since she had not spoken aloud. Chief Justice Shaw, no doubt anticipating the challenge, made a detailed ruling that any form of communication should be considered speech, and therefore, the evidence should be presented to the jury, along with testimony by other witnesses that Angeline Taylor was conscious and displayed a knowledge and understanding of her situation and surroundings even if unable to speak.

One wonders if Butler instead might have challenged the evidence on the grounds that she had only been asked a single question—if Casey had been

After representing Thomas Casey, Benjamin F. Butler (1818–1893) went on to serve as a general in the Civil War, congressman and governor of Massachusetts during his colorful career. *Courtesy of the Missouri History Museum.*

the murderer. Perhaps she had just heard "squeeze my hand" and might have responded the same way if she had been asked, for example, if the family cat had been the murderer? In any case, the point went uncontested.

After the prosecution rested, Butler declined to call any witnesses. He did, however, bring up a point of law. The indictment specified that Casey was to be tried for the murder of Angelina Taylor, yet every witness had referred to her as "Angeline," and therefore the government had failed to prove its case. This motion was a classic Butler maneuver, searching for a technical or procedural error on the part of the prosecution to throw out their entire case. Attorney General Choate immediately leapt to his feet to respond that if there was any doubt, then either or both of Angelina's parents could be recalled to testify on the matter. Butler responded that Choate's offer to recall witnesses after the prosecution had rested was an admission that they had failed to prove their case and that the prisoner should be released.

Justice Shaw was not impressed by Butler's assertion. "The Courts of this State, for several years, had had a tendency to do away with the old technicalities which fetter their proceedings," he intoned. By not challenging the identity of Angeline Taylor during the presentation of the prosecution's case, Butler had in effect conceded that point of fact. To ensure that the rights of the prisoner were not infringed, however, Shaw would allow further testimony to clarify that Angelina and Angeline were indeed the same person. Butler had lost, and he knew it. He still wouldn't concede the point, however, either because it was his last chance to muddy the waters for the prosecution or because to back down now would be an admission that his point of law had been nothing but a cynical gambit. "Now that your Honor has re-opened the case for the government," Butler inquired, "I suppose you will allow me time to obtain the family Bible, to ascertain by that what her name was—"

Shaw immediately cut him off. "Mr. Butler, what do you *mean*? Do you intend to insult the Court?"

Butler responded calmly in a pleasant tone. "I had no such intention, your honor."

"Why then did you say the Court had opened the case *for the government*?" interjected Shaw, his face now flushed red with indignation.

"I only meant that the court had opened the case for the introduction of testimony by the government."

"Did you mean nothing more?" asked Shaw, still not satisfied with Butler's intentions.

"That was all, upon my honor," Butler answered and then added, very slowly and mischievously, "What else *could* I mean?"

Rufus Choate
(1799–1859) was
attorney general
of Massachusetts
when he assisted
in the prosecution
of Thomas Casey.
*Courtesy of the Harvard
Fogg Museum.*

"If that was all, I am satisfied," Shaw responded, ready to drop the matter. Butler was heard to say under his breath, "So am I."

After several witnesses testified that Angelina and Angeline were indeed one and the same person, the government rested again. Butler again declined to call any witnesses, and Justice Shaw turned to the prisoner in the dock. "Mr. Casey, if you have anything to say to the Jury, you may do so." At first, Casey shrank back into his chair, as if to disappear. After a few moments, he slowly rose. There he stood, lips trembling, eyes cast downward, for what seemed to observers to have been several minutes. Finally, Butler whispered to Casey and then told the court that his client had nothing to say. Shaw then gave his charge to the jury, a ninety-minute lecture on the law and the salient points of the case. In his summary, Shaw stated that there was no evidence found on Casey tying him to the crime, nor did the prosecution establish a motive. The evidence came down to the testimony of Mrs. Taylor's condition at the time of her "dying declaration" and of the credibility of the witnesses relating Casey's confession at the Lowell jail in February. After three days of testimony, the case was now in the hands of the jury.

After only twenty minutes, the court reconvened. As Casey stood listening, Shaw turned to the foreman, Benjamin F. Holden of Lowell, and asked if the jury had reached a verdict. "Yes, your honor," responded Holden. "Guilty."

Sentence was passed the following day. Casey again declined to speak, and Justice Shaw declared that for the crime of willful murder, he would be hanged by the neck until dead. Casey's was the first capital case after the passage of a new state law providing for a minimum waiting time of one year between sentence and execution, during which time he would be confined at the Charlestown State Prison. He met his end at the East Cambridge jail yard on October 5, 1854. The gallows were covered with a canvas awning, so none but the required witnesses and officials could see the execution. Thomas Casey was attended to in his cell by Father O'Brien of the Franklin Street Catholic Church in Boston, and he was escorted out to the yard at 10:00 a.m. With the noose placed on Casey, Middlesex County sheriff John Keyes read the death warrant. Casey declined his last opportunity to speak, and at 10:17 a.m., the trapdoor beneath him was released. After twenty minutes, physicians examining him determined he was still alive, and he was left to hang another forty minutes before being declared dead.

The orphaned Taylor children grew up with their Davis grandparents in Sherborn, Massachusetts. Ella Edna Taylor, the baby who had been found lying next to her mother in the parlor, died from croup a little over a year later, on October 7, 1853. The other three children survived into adulthood. Ouvra Jr. never married and died at the age of seventy-two in Leominster, Massachusetts, in 1917. Rosabella Taylor, the child who was found still asleep upstairs by Alfred Taylor, married Horace Stratton, had six children and died in Sherborn in 1911 at the age of sixty-one. Eldest daughter Agnes Taylor married George F. Ward and had four children. When she died in Natick at the age of eighty-six on March 31, 1934, she was the final witness to the events of that horrible morning eighty-two years earlier.

4

WEST NATICK, 1899

THE *OTHER* MORSE FAMILY, PART 1

The name Morse is well-known in Natick. There was Mary Ann (Stone) Morse, who in her will endowed a hospital (opened 1899) named for her late husband, Leonard. There's also the Morse Institute Library (opened 1873), named in honor of Samuel Morse (not to be confused with the inventor of the telegraph) and endowed by his granddaughter, a different Mary Ann Morse. (She was Leonard's fifth cousin once removed.) But there was a third branch of the Morse family who lived in Natick, certainly less eminent but perhaps even more intriguing.

Willard Morse (1811–1871) was a prosperous farmer who lived in a big house on Speen Street. He was a nephew of the Samuel Morse who started the first library in town and for whom the Morse Institute Library was named. Willard married Mary Nichols and had eleven children. After his death in 1871, the five children who never married continued to live in the house with their widowed mother and operate the farm. These were Willard Warren (born 1839), Electa A. (born 1844), Rufus B. (born 1850), Ira Herbert (born 1854) and Lizzie H. (born 1855).

By the mid-1890s, the family had already developed a reputation for eccentricity. Electa embarked on a series of lawsuits that made headlines, challenging the wills of first, her uncle Rufus Morse, who died in 1893; second, her aunt Caroline (Morse) Hayes, who died in 1895; and third, her aunt Maria G. (Morse) Hayes, who died in 1900. In each instance, Electa acted as her own attorney. The contest over her uncle Rufus's will turned on the mysterious appearance of a second will seemingly out of nowhere that later proved to be a forgery. In 1896, the Massachusetts Supreme Judicial Court justice presiding over the appeal of the Caroline Hayes case admonished Electa that "it seemed that she was asking questions for the sake of giving pain to the witness" and to frame them properly. (That justice, none other than Oliver Wendell Holmes Jr., would be appointed to the United State Supreme Court six years later.)

Though well off, the Morses lived "primitively," which in the 1890s meant that they went without modern conveniences such as electricity, telephone or even running water. The elder two brothers were in poor health and never left the house, with all the business of the estate handled by youngest brother, Ira.

Four days before Christmas 1899, Ira was in Waltham conducting business, leaving his four siblings and mother at home. In the mid-afternoon, Electa, then forty-five years old, started walking down Speen Street to the village of Walkerville to fetch some things for her mother when she spotted two men, Louis A. Perry and Arnold Stappen, on bicycles headed north. They called out to her "using insulting language" from a distance, and their catcalls only increased as she turned around to head back to the safety of her home. By the time she reached the door, she shouted that she was being pursued and urged her brother Rufus to bolt it behind her. Through the window, Rufus could see the two men, both in their thirties, carrying their bicycles and then throwing them down on the lawn in front of the house. As Electa ran upstairs sobbing, her mother asked through the door what the men wanted. "We want the girls, give us the girls!" Stappen then raised a fist up to the glass and yelled in a German accent, "Let us in or we will smash the glass!" Perry, meanwhile, ran to the door in the ell of the house, but Rufus had gotten there first and bolted it. Then Perry raced around to the windows on the north side of the house and tried to open them, but they were locked. This standoff continued until the men outside grabbed rocks from the stone wall and began throwing them through the Morses' windows. Perry even managed to lob one through a window on the second floor, narrowly missing Electa. A game of whack-a-mole ensued, with Perry and Stappen trying to gain entrance to the house at various points while being repelled by the Morse siblings.

Finally, Perry broke a drawing room window behind Lizzie's prized piano and, given a boost by Stappen, gained entrance and pushed the piano backward before the Morses could reach the other side. Perry lunged toward Electa, grabbing her around the neck. Lizzie, wielding a croquet mallet in one hand and a revolver in the other, confronted Perry.

He scoffed, saying he had served in Cuba in the last war, and he wasn't afraid of a pistol. He let go of Electa and wrenched the mallet from Lizzie's hands, striking her down. She fell at the foot of the stairs. Perry lunged forward, but Rufus grabbed him from behind and shouted to his sister, "Give it to him!" Lizzie fired four shots in quick succession, all of which providentially missed her brother, although three also missed Perry. The fourth, however, struck him squarely in the chest. "You've shot me," he cried. "I'll not die a coward!" With that, Perry leapt out through a window onto the front lawn and collapsed in a heap.

Stappen called to him to get his wheel so they might leave, but Perry said he could not and asked his friend to stretch his body out straight so that he might die in a dignified position. After doing so, Stappen again went to pound on the front door, demanding he be let in. After a few minutes, he took to his bicycle and pedaled off. Charles Bowen, a hired hand who worked for John Walker about a half mile away, arrived just as Stappen departed. Bowen later told police that earlier in the afternoon Perry and Stappen had jumped from their bikes and tried to rob him before they

The attack on the Morse home was front-page news in Boston. Boston Globe, *courtesy of Newspapers.com.*

went to the Morses'. Stappen returned a while later with a Mr. Pulsifer and an express wagon to retrieve Perry's body, at which time he was arrested.

Why Perry and Stappen had seemingly gone mad that day puzzled authorities. Both were married, and Stappen had three children. Stappen had emigrated from Germany, settling first in South Dakota before coming to Natick in 1892. He had worked for J.B. Fiske's hardware store prior to getting a job as a collection agent for a Boston life insurance company. He and Perry had had a couple of glasses of wine and then set off up Speen Street to make premium collections in Wayland. Perry had served in the Sixth Massachusetts Regiment in the Spanish-American War and worked as a printer at the Dennison Manufacturing Company in South Framingham. Neither had had any previous run-ins with the law. Stappen pleaded guilty and was sentenced to three and a half years in prison for his part in the assault on the Morse home. (Lizzie Morse was investigated for manslaughter, but ultimately, the charges were dropped.)

The traumas of that day only increased the Morses' reluctance to engage with the outside world. Ira continued to run the farm, and Electa continued to pursue her lawsuits. In February 1910, Electa again made the newspapers when she accused Natick police chief Peter G. Klein of assault. The incident stemmed from the attempts of John L. Shaw of the Natick moth department to access the Morse farm to destroy cocoons on the property. He and his men were run off the property by Electa, who claimed they were trespassing. The next week, Shaw returned with Chief Klein, who assured Electa that by town ordinance, the town had the right to venture onto her farm in the interest of destroying pernicious moth colonies. While negotiations ensued for a long period, Shaw was eventually allowed to do his job. Chief Klein was surprised to learn several days later that Electa had gone before the selectmen to accuse him of striking her. After another prolonged discussion, Electa conceded that the chief, in fact, might not have struck her and allowed that she had "dreamed a man would call at the house that day and attack the inmates." Still, one can't help but feel sympathy for Electa given her previous experience.

Willard Warren Morse died in 1913, and after Ira Morse died the following year, the family's contact with the outside world ceased. Other than the Fitts Brothers food deliveries, no one was allowed on the farm. One of the sisters would travel to the town hall once a year to pay the family's taxes with absurdly outdated currency, but that would be the only time they were seen in Natick. Rumors spread that vast sums of money were stored in the house. In fact, by the 1920s, the Morse siblings were on the town welfare rolls, as even Lizzie, the youngest, had reached her seventies.

The spring of 1927 was a dry one in Natick, and on April 20, a brushfire broke out along Speen Street. It flared, jumping the road to the Morse property, where the dense underbrush of the abandoned farm provided ample fuel, and soon, winds carried flames to the roof of the house itself. The West Natick fire company arrived on the scene. As soon as they opened the front door, they encountered Rufus on a mattress in the front hall, unable to walk. He was immediately sent in an ambulance to Leonard Morse Hospital. The firefighters made their way through the home filled knee-deep with debris. The kitchen floor was entirely covered with pots, pans and crockery, much of it broken. Eventually, they found Electa and Lizzie upstairs fighting flames with buckets of water, stubbornly independent to the end, joined by a third sister. Sarah (Morse) Tibbetts, who had moved back into the house following the death of her husband. After much coaxing, the Morse sisters were finally persuaded to leave the job to the professionals and were taken off, still protesting, to the Natick poor farm. As soon as the flames were extinguished, crowds of curious neighbors descended on the house, intent on picking up a souvenir or perhaps digging through the ruins for treasure. Police had to be stationed on the property around the clock to prevent looting.

The next day, the sisters returned to salvage what they could. Newspaper reporters joined to view what was essentially a one-hundred-year-old time capsule. There were flintlock muskets and powder horns from the Revolution, rich mahogany Federal-style furniture, whale oil lamps, plates commemorating the laying of the cornerstone of the Bunker Hill Monument by General Lafayette in 1825, a paper box containing a piece of wedding cake and a china Puritan cradle that had been given to a young Electa by Henry Wilson, a neighbor who went on to serve as a senator and vice president of the United States. Electa told a reporter from the *Boston Globe* that she had studied law and even once assisted Supreme Court justice Oliver Wendell Holmes. (True, if by "assisted" she meant "annoyed.")

Rufus died in the hospital, but the three sisters continued to live in the Natick poorhouse for the remainder of their lives. Town officials, however, became incensed about a year after their arrival, when it was discovered, through bank books found sewn into their blankets, that the sisters had a then significant sum of $30,000 in various accounts. The selectmen informed the sisters that they would have to leave, but they refused. The town farm had become their home. A compromise was reached when a conservator, appointed over their objections, paid the town rent from their savings. Electa, the last of the sisters, died at the age of eighty-five in 1931. But this "other" Morse family of Natick had not yet ended its colorful adventures, as we shall see in a later chapter.

5

FRAMINGHAM, 1902

CALLER IN THE NIGHT

O n Saturday, May 17, 1902, eleven-year-old Beatrice Emery was in her upstairs apartment on Hartford Street in Framingham around 8:00 p.m., when she heard the doorbell ring. She quickly ran downstairs to answer, not wanting to disturb her mother, Josephine. The Emery family had moved to Framingham just two years before in an effort to improve the ailing Josephine's health. A surprise visitor on a Saturday night would do nothing but aggravate Mrs. Emery's already fragile nerves.

When Beatrice opened the door, she was surprised to see what appeared to be a young girl around her own age or even slightly younger. But as Beatrice looked more closely in the darkening night, she realized that the visitor, despite being only about three and a half feet tall, was not a young girl but a woman in her twenties or perhaps older. The woman asked to speak with Beatrice's father, thirty-two-year-old Andrew Jackson Emery Jr. Beatrice replied that her father had ridden his bike to the village and should be home shortly. The visitor told Beatrice that when her father returned, he was to go and speak with his neighbor Mr. Dunn about an important matter. She then turned and left, and Beatrice went back upstairs to tell her mother.

Nearly two hours later, the doorbell rang again, followed by a loud commotion that woke Beatrice from her sleep. As she rushed to the stairs, she was startled by the unfamiliar, unexpected yet unmistakable sound of gunshots coming from the front door at the bottom of the stairs. The scene Beatrice witnessed as she came to the top of the stairs was horrifying. Her mother was standing on the stairway screaming. Her father lay

Above: Andrew Emery and his family lived on the northwest corner of Hartford Street and Harrison Street in the Lokerville section of Framingham, as seen on this map. *Courtesy of Framingham History Center.*

Right: The house on Hartford Street, where Andrew Emery was shot, 2020. *Photo by author.*

crumpled in his nightshirt at the bottom of the stairs, bleeding from his chin and midsection.

Outside, the diminutive visitor from earlier in the evening stood calmly on the porch while neighbors rushed to the scene. William F. Dunn, Eugene Westcott and Edward Cotter were first to arrive, rushing from Mr. Dunn's house, where they had been gathered in the parlor. The men quickly took in the situation and realized that two things were evident: Andrew Emery was dying from gunshot wounds and the shooter was the tiny woman standing calmly on the front porch. Cotter ran to telephone for a doctor while Dunn comforted the hysterical Mrs. Emery. The grief-stricken wife screamed out, "She did it, she's the one!" indicating the woman standing on the piazza. The woman made no attempt to escape or deny the accusation.

Several more neighbors arrived in the next few minutes, accompanying the shocked Mrs. Emery back upstairs to be with Beatrice and her other three children. One of the new arrivals, Michael Cahill, began to interrogate the young woman.

"Did you do this?" Cahill asked.

"Yes," she replied with no emotion.

"Why did you do this?"

"I don't know" was the answer.

As Cahill's questioning became more intense, Dunn and Westcott advised the woman to stay silent on the matter for the moment. But Cahill persisted, asking her what she had done with the weapon. The woman said she had thrown it into the grass bordering the house. A search by Cahill in the grass where the woman had indicated yielded a small .22-caliber handgun.

The scene remained eerily quiet while the group waited for the arrival of a doctor and the police. Within minutes, Framingham police chief Robert S. Place arrived with Dr. William R. Morrow. During his questioning, the chief established the identity of the woman as twenty-two-year-old Nina Frances Danforth of West Newton. The woman's petite stature undoubtedly added to the surreal atmosphere of the scene on Hartford Street that night. While later news articles would describe her in a variety of ways that would surely offend twenty-first-century readers ("deformed and dwarfed," a "tiny hunchbacked midget," the "hideous distorted figure of vengeance," a "little dwarfed child-girl" with "a face as beautiful as her body is deformed"), it is difficult to accurately assess the cause of Nina's physical condition. Most likely, she suffered from some type of birth defect of the spine that stunted her growth and made her susceptible to other ailments, including severe headaches.

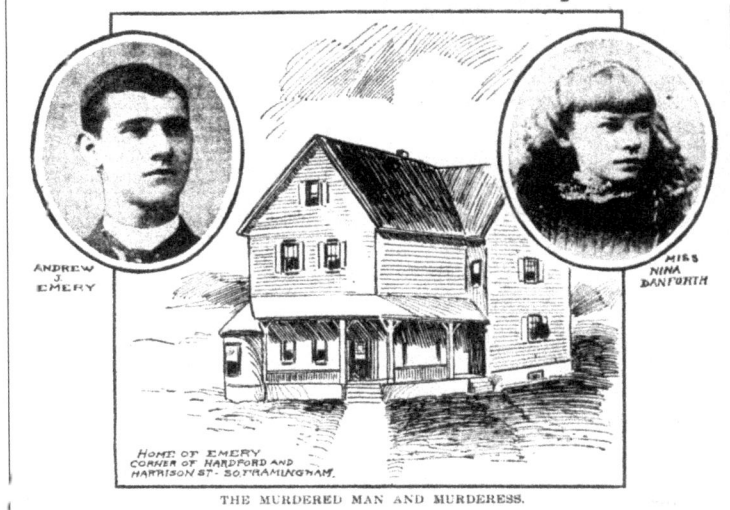

Nina Danforth Refuses to Tell Why She Murdered Andrew Emery.

ANDREW
J.
EMERY

MISS
NINA
DANFORTH

HOME OF EMERY AND
CORNER OF HARDFORD AND
HARRISON ST. SO FRAMINGHAM.

THE MURDERED MAN AND MURDERESS.

The salacious details of the Nina Danforth story made it front-page news around the country for weeks. This illustration from the *Boston Globe* ran the day after the murder. Boston Globe, *courtesy of Newspapers.com.*

Danforth readily admitted to shooting Andrew Emery, but when her motive was questioned by the chief, she again replied, "I don't know." Dr. Morrow was worried about Danforth's mental and physical condition, so he engaged a carriage and accompanied her, along with the chief, to the Old Colony Hotel near the depot.

A nurse by the name of Miss Fair was called to tend to the fragile widow Emery, while the late Mr. Emery was transported to undertaker Smith's, where an autopsy would be performed by Dr. Morrow and medical examiner William Richards of Natick. Nina Danforth was left under guard at the hotel, and Chief Place was left with a number of unanswered questions, most puzzling of which was why this twenty-two-year-old woman would bring sudden and violent death in the middle of the night to a young family man.

Over the next few days, the Emery family would bid a sad goodbye to their husband and father and prepare his body for burial in his native Vermont. Nina Danforth was transferred by train to a jail cell in Cambridge, awaiting arraignment on a charge of murder. As she lay suffering from headaches and other maladies in her cell, the sordid details of the relationship between Nina and Andrew Emery came to light and were shared with an eager and curious public in newspapers across the country.

It could be said that the thirty-two-year-old father and husband and the twenty-two-year-old woman "met cute." Emery worked as a firefighter for the Boston and Albany Railroad, stoking the steam engines on the locomotive that made daily runs from Framingham to Boston. The rail line passed through West Newton across from Washington Street, where Nina's house stood facing the tracks. What began as a friendly wave each day from Emery to the young woman standing on her porch eventually turned into a more intimate relationship when Emery alighted from the train in West Newton and paid Nina a call at her home in the fall of 1900. According to Nina's parents and neighbors, Emery was an occasional visitor over the next year and a half, bringing small tokens and affectionate letters to the young woman, the entire time presenting himself as a single man interested in more than a passing friendship.

Perhaps the most shocking detail of the affair was Nina's claim that she and Emery had been secretly married months before the shooting and had spent a three-day honeymoon at a hotel in Boston. O.F. Schuehle, proprietor of the Appleton House on Tremont Street, distinctly remembered the couple spending a weekend at the hotel in October 1901, stating, "I should not have recognized Emery as the man if he had been alone, but the appearance of his companion imprinted both very strong in my memory." This honeymoon, according to Nina, began the day after their marriage somewhere near Castle Square in the South End. Emery had even produced an official-looking marriage license but had cautioned Nina to keep the marriage a secret for the time being, until he was able to live with her as a proper spouse. In the meantime, they met frequently after his workday ended and regularly exchanged passionate letters.

While Nina might not have been happy with this arrangement, she tolerated it and trusted that the day would arrive when she and Andrew Emery could be together. She simply had to look at the portrait in her watchcase that Emery had given her to keep hope alive in her heart. Just when and how Nina discovered that her lover was a married man is unclear. Some friends stated she had known for several months, others said she

From this house on Washington Street in West Newton, Nina Danforth first became acquainted with Andrew Emery. *Photo by author.*

had known for several weeks and still others claimed she found out on the morning of the shooting via a letter from Emery.

According to family members, Nina received a letter that Saturday morning that caused her great distress. After reading it, she left the house in a hurry. Some witnesses claimed that Nina went to South Station looking for Emery, while others say she took the train directly to Framingham. What is known is that she arrived at the Framingham Station on Waverly Street in downtown at about 8:00 p.m. She was carrying her brother's Spanish-American War service revolver that she had taken from his room, as well as a bottle of laudanum, with which she might have been planning to dispatch herself after confronting Emery. Nina caught a trolley for the mile-long trip down Concord Street to Hartford Street. Later, several witnesses saw Nina standing in some bushes, apparently waiting for Emery to return from his errands. Heated words were exchanged, and Emery went into his home. Several hours later, Nina made her second, fateful call to the house.

Much of this information was given in testimony by the twenty-five witnesses who were called at an inquest in Framingham on May 23, presided

The Boston and Albany station on Waverly Street in Framingham. *Courtesy of Framingham History Center.*

over by Judge Willis Kingsbury. Nina's family had retained the services of Franz Hugo Krebs, a prominent Boston lawyer who had served with Nina's brother Arthur in Cuba. A number of witnesses appeared, including Chief Place; various Emery neighbors; Beatrice Emery; O.F. Schuehle, proprietor of the Appleton House in Boston; and Nina's brother John and his wife, Bessie. Nina was held in the East Cambridge Jail after the hearing but returned by train to Framingham for a subsequent hearing, traveling on the same line where Andrew Emery had worked and passing by her family home where the two had met in happier times.

On June 2, the grand jury met in Cambridge District Court to decide what criminal charges, if any, Nina would face. The same witnesses who had testified at the inquest in Framingham appeared again. After the Danforth family members testified to the fragile condition of Nina's physical and emotional health, Middlesex County district attorney George Sanderson had to remind the jury that they were to consider only the bare facts of the case. Despite their growing sympathy for the woman and their inclination to pass on any criminal charges, the fact remained that she had shot a man in cold blood in his own home in front of his wife and child. If no indictment was brought against her that day, she would walk free. A murder indictment would allow the extenuating circumstances of the crime to be considered

Pleads Not Guilty to Murder and Is Held for Hearing

NINA DANFORTH IN HER CELL IN THE CAMBRIDGE JAIL.

Depictions such as this from the front page of the *Boston Post* made Nina more sympathetic to the public. Boston Post, *courtesy of Newspapers.com.*

and would allow Nina to be examined by an alienist to determine her state of mind at the time of the shooting. Sanderson's efforts paid off, and an indictment of first-degree murder was returned against Nina.

Nina remained in her cell during the testimony and was not immediately told of the indictment for fear that her deteriorating condition would worsen on hearing the news. A large crowd including mothers with young children in tow had been gathering outside the jail eating picnic lunches under the trees while waiting to catch a glimpse of the young murderess. Shortly before 4:00 p.m., Nina stepped out of the jail and, flanked by her sister and Middlesex County sheriff John Fairbairn, walked across the street to the court to hear the charge and enter her plea. A little more than five minutes later, she returned to her cell after pleading "not guilty."

Nina's initial admission of guilt and the eyewitness testimony to the crime left little in the way of a defense strategy, other than pleading insanity or accepting a plea to a lesser charge. Over the course of that summer, Nina met regularly with Dr. Edward Utley, the jail physician, to determine her state of mind. Massachusetts attorney general Herbert Parker closely monitored Utley's progress with the prisoner. In August, Dr. Utley determined that Nina was indeed sane, both now and at the time of the shooting. Her defense team would now have to consider a plea to a lesser charge.

Support for Nina was building across the country, thanks in part to the relentless press coverage of every aspect of the case. After a search of Emery's work locker, the *Boston Post* reported that it contained "dime novels of the type usually favored by boys of 12 years," while "in contradiction from Emery's taste in literature, Miss Danforth's was very refined in her selection of reading matter. She enjoyed the standard magazines and read the better class of novels." Nina's physical disability alone made her a pitiful

Sheriff Fairbairn, Nina Danforth and Her Sister, on Their Way from the Jail to the Court House. Miss Danforth in the Center.

Nina Danforth walking to court, escorted by her sister and the ubiquitous Sheriff John Fairbairn. Boston Globe, *courtesy of Newspapers.com.*

figure in the public eye, and the perfidy of a scoundrel such as Emery only increased their sympathy and desire for a lenient punishment, if any.

The district attorney recognized that putting Nina on trial would not only be unpopular with the public but might even result in an acquittal, so a plea bargain was offered. On November 12, Nina pled guilty to manslaughter. During his summary of the case for the court, District Attorney George Sanderson emphasized Nina's physical disabilities and sufferings, as well as her resulting emotional immaturity, describing her as "a woman in years" but "less than a child in development." Attorney Arthur Johnson, speaking on Nina's behalf, summarized her plight by saying, "As she grew up she was taught by her mother that love in its ordinary sense was impossible for her. The manner in which she found love and was taught to love was a most severe shock to her sensitive nature." Nina did not speak and appeared emotionless during the hearing, as she had during previous court appearances. However, she had consistently shown remorse and regret when questioned by reporters, declaring her love for Andrew Emery even after she had taken his life. Nina was sentenced to twenty-one months to be served in the Middlesex House of Correction. This seemed like an appropriate solution for a prosecution reluctant to try a handicapped young woman whom many felt was justified in her actions. After an article appeared in the *Globe* that December describing Nina's participation in a jailhouse Christmas play, the story faded from the headlines.

While the press and the public might have forgotten her, her family and defense counsel did not. Almost from the moment of her conviction, they had been working on a petition for Nina's pardon, citing her deteriorating physical condition and emotional suffering due to her incarceration. Since her arrest, Nina had suffered regular headaches, and it was argued that the heat of the coming summer months would further weaken her. With little opposition, save from the Emery family, the petition went to Governor John Bates, who signed the pardon on June 11, 1903. The next day, Nina walked out of the East Cambridge jail and spoke briefly to the press, thanking the governor, Sheriff Fairbairn and his assistants and the newspapers that had supported her. She had served seven months of her twenty-one-month sentence.

After a short stay at her sister's house in Medford, Nina returned to Newton and tried to move on from the events of the past year. But just a few years later, she was making headlines again in a situation that was all too familiar. In April 1908, Nina was back in court, charged with sending a threatening letter to a Newton woman named Emma Palmer.

Nina and Palmer had a history; two years earlier, they had been involved in a shouting match on Washington Street near the post office, during which Palmer called her a "hussy," and Nina swore she would get even. Nina reported the incident to police, but no charges were filed against either woman. The bad blood between the two had stemmed from Nina's "keeping company" with Palmer's husband, Frank, a charge both Nina and Frank denied.

The letter that landed Nina in front of Judge Frank M. Copeland read in part: "Shame on the dirty trick," "I will avenge it" and "Beware!" Although the letter was unsigned, Judge Copeland believed that Nina had indeed written it and had intended it as a threat to Mrs. Palmer. Palmer, however, admitted that she felt no fear of bodily harm from Nina, and the case was dismissed.

During questioning, Prosecutor Fletcher asked Nina if she was on probation, referencing the Andrew Emery case, to which Nina responded that she had been pardoned in that case. Nina's counsel, Thomas Vahey, summarized by saying, "What happened to Miss Danforth she has taken as a lesson that she cannot harm anyone without being punished." It was a lesson that she apparently heeded, for there is no record of any more court appearances by her. Nina might have yet found the love that her attorney described as "impossible" for her to experience. On March 4, 1915, Nina (now using her middle name of Frances) married Harrison Clark, a factory manager twenty years her senior, in Boston. The couple moved to Medford and were together for five years before Nina died on December 11, 1920.

6

WESTON, 1904

THE SPINSTER ON SOUTH AVENUE

In the early twentieth century, Edward Page was a respected businessman living on South Avenue in Weston with his adult children, Harold and Mabel. Although he was prosperous at one time, personal and financial troubles had befallen the seventy-seven-year-old, forcing him to give up his residence on Commonwealth Avenue in Boston and move to the family's "summer home." In the course of just a few short years, the Page family experienced a series of tragedies that would have tested the fortitude of any family. In 1897, the elder son, Edward Jr., after losing a fortune in an investment scheme, disappeared off a steamship returning from New York. Two years after that, Mr. Page's sister disappeared from her Auburndale home and was later found drowned in the Charles River. The most devastating was the death in 1902 of Page's beloved wife, Elizabeth, an event that left unmarried forty-one-year-old Mabel in a melancholic state. On March 31, 1904, tragedy would once again visit the unfortunate family.

On that Thursday before Easter, Edward Page left his home early in the morning to perform a few errands. Harold Page was at his job at South Station, where he worked as a freight agent for the Boston and Albany Railroad. His sister, Mabel, remained at home in the sprawling house on South Avenue in the eastern part of town. On arriving home around 2:30 p.m., Edward noticed that the front door was slightly ajar. He entered the house and called to his daughter, with no response. Failing to find her downstairs, Page climbed the stairs to Mabel's bedroom, where he made a gruesome discovery. Mabel was lying on her back beside the bed, clearly

The Edward Page house on South Avenue, Weston, 2020. *Photo by author.*

deceased. Edward frantically ran to the homes of several neighbors, one of whom called the medical examiner, Dr. Julian Meade.

Meade arrived and did a cursory inspection of the body, finding wounds to Mabel's chest and neck, leading him to conclude that it was a case of suicide, though no weapon was found. It wasn't until ten o'clock that night, when undertaker John Bruce went to remove the body from the bedroom floor and discovered stab wounds between the shoulder blades, that it was clear that a murder had been committed. Just why anyone would want to bring harm to this well-loved and respected middle-aged woman was a mystery. She had not been sexually assaulted, and there were no signs of any valuables missing from the house. A note in Mabel's handwriting, discovered by Edward Page on a table just inside the front doorway, offered a clue about how an intruder could have gained access to the house, if not why: "Harold has been injured and has been taken to the Massachusetts General Hospital in Boston. I am going in there on the 12:00 train. You will find the key in the barn."

When Harold Page arrived at the Weston home unharmed late in the afternoon, it was suggested that some trusted acquaintance of Mabel's had

Mabel Page. *Boston Post*, *courtesy of Newspapers.com.*

used the false story to gain access into the house. Worried citizens from Weston and beyond, fueled by sensational headlines in the Boston papers, panicked. There was widespread fear that some "lunatic," "maniac," "half-wit," "degenerate" or "tramp" was wandering the countryside waiting to strike again. A $500 reward was offered by the Weston selectmen for information leading to the arrest of the killer.

Over that Easter weekend, police, the press and curiosity seekers descended on the Page estate and the surrounding neighborhood, and the police weren't the only ones actively trying to solve the mystery. On Saturday, April 2, a persistent *Boston Post* photographer was continually being thwarted by police from taking a photo of the rear of the Page home. Undeterred, he crossed a neighboring property and sloughed through a shallow brook to get the shot. There in the water, he discovered a jackknife with a dark stain that seemed to be blood. The *Post* then did the responsible thing and turned the knife over to authorities—only after photographing it and running the photo (actual size) on page one of the Sunday edition. To further the claim that it was indeed the murder weapon, a *Post* reporter purchased a similar knife to do his own forensic investigation. After procuring a hind quarter of beef from the Mayo Meat Company in Boston, he repeatedly stabbed it to prove that the knife that was found could have inflicted the wounds on Mabel Page.

Not to be outdone by its rival *Post*, the *Globe* got in on the detecting business as well. While canvassing for witnesses who might have been in the area at the time of the murder, the name of Charles Tucker came to the attention of *Globe* reporters. Tucker was twenty-three, unemployed and living with his parents in Auburndale. He had once worked at the Riverside boathouse and was known to take long walks throughout Newton Lower Falls and Weston. In a *Globe* interview, Tucker described the route of his wanderings on the day of the murder, admitting that he had come within a third of a mile of the Page house, stopping at an intersection known as Cutter's Corner, before turning and heading back to Auburndale. He concluded the interview by saying, "I wish that I might be able to give some information that would lead to the detection of the murderer, but I saw nothing. It was a fearful thing."

THE FATEFUL HOURS OF MARCH 31 AT THE PAGE HOME IN WESTON

The *Boston Post* offered this creative timeline of the Page murder. The Page home is pictured in the center of the clock. Boston Post, *courtesy of Newspapers.com.*

The state police read the interview and were very interested in speaking with Tucker for several reasons. First, he fit the profile of someone who was in the area at the time of the murder and knew the family. Tucker had once worked with Harold Page at the Boston and Albany Railroad and, according to Harold, had been to the house on at least one occasion to purchase a dog and had been introduced to Mabel. In the interview, Tucker claimed no personal acquaintance with the Page family. While his unsavory reputation would not categorize him as the "maniac" or "half-wit" that the public had deemed responsible for the brutal crime, it was sullied enough for police to consider him a suspect. He had been dismissed from his job at the Riverside boathouse after getting caught forging checks. He had also been accused of stealing from a cash box. Most damning were the rumors about his involvement in the April 1903 drowning death of his wife of five months, Louise. According to Tucker, while canoeing on the Charles, the couple tipped the boat while switching positions, throwing them both into the water. Louise Tucker was unable to swim and was supported by her husband for as long as he could, until she slipped away from his arms. To many, Tucker's story seemed implausible, considering that the incident occurred in just four feet of water. Few people who knew Tucker, including friends and his own father-in-law, believed that it was an accident.

Tucker was questioned by police for four hours and then released the day after the interview appeared in the *Globe*. However, he was arrested five days later, with state police chief Joseph Shaw announcing, "We believe we have the right man." Tucker was arraigned in Waltham District Court on April 11, represented by James Vahey of the law firm of Vahey and Innes. (James's partner and brother Thomas Vahey would later represent Nina Danforth in her 1908 court appearance for threatening Emma Palmer.) A large crowd had gathered to watch the proceedings, with several young women in the crowd carrying bouquets in hopes of giving them to the accused. Over the next few months, Tucker and his parents would receive hundreds of letters of support, many of which contained cash contributions to help with his defense. Continued investigations by local and state police furnished enough evidence to bring to the grand jury, and Tucker was indicted on June 16 for first-degree murder. In November, the trial date was set for January 2, 1905.

The day after New Year's saw a large crowd gathered in East Cambridge to get a glimpse of the defendant as he walked from the jail to the courthouse, accompanied by Middlesex sheriff John Fairbairn, who had performed the same duty three years earlier with Nina Danforth. Tucker remained expressionless, even after the crowd let out a loud cheer. Inside the courthouse, Tucker stepped into the ornate prisoner's cage and turned to face the presiding judges, Judge Edgar Sherman and Judge Henry V. Sheldon. Representing the state were Attorney General Herbert Parker and Middlesex County district attorney George Sanderson. Jury selection was completed on the first day, and the twelve men accompanied by both the prosecution and defense teams boarded a special trolley to Newton to tour several sites associated with the case. Their first stop was the home of Charles Tucker, followed by a trip to the Page house and the murder scene in Mabel's bedroom.

One of the first witnesses called was Dr. Julian Meade, the medical examiner who had at first declared the murder a suicide. Early twentieth-century forensics being what they were, Dr. Meade demonstrated the location and severity of Page's wounds using a human female skeleton he brought with him. It was reported that Tucker took a keen interest in Dr. Meade's demonstration.

The prosecution presented several pieces of evidence that incriminated Tucker and supported a motive of robbery. A slip of paper found in Mabel Page's bedroom by the body with the words "J.L. Morton, Charlestown" was believed to have been left by Tucker. A single-edge knife (not, alas, the one found by the *Boston Post*) believed to be the murder weapon was found in his room, along with a stickpin bearing a Canadian shield. The knife blade had been broken into three pieces, indicating Tucker's attempts to conceal the damning evidence. Other prosecution witnesses included:

- Handwriting experts who testified that "without a doubt" Tucker had written the "J.L. Morton" note.
- Amy Roberts, the Pages' maid, who identified the Canadian stickpin found on Tucker as belonging to Mabel Page. She also testified that ten dollars was missing from Mabel's purse.
- State police chief Shaw, who confirmed that the broken knife was found in Tucker's room and that Tucker admitted he had broken it for fear he would become a suspect in the case. Shaw also identified a knife sheath that fit Tucker's knife that was found in a peddler's cart in which he had ridden the day of the murder.
- Local residents who had seen Tucker in the area of the Page home around the presumed time of the attack. There were no eyewitnesses who could place the defendant on South Avenue, but the witness accounts contradicted Tucker's own version of his travels that day.

After twelve days of testimony, the commonwealth rested its case on January 14.

Vahey and his defense team refuted all of the state's evidence and witness testimony. They called expert witnesses who testified that the murder weapon had to have been a double-edge blade, not a single-edge one like the one Tucker possessed. They produced their own handwriting experts who claimed the "J.L. Morton" note was not written by Tucker but by Mabel Page herself. Witnesses were produced who had seen Charles Tucker wearing the Canadian stickpin in his hat several years before the murder.

SCENE IN COURTROOM AT EAST CAMBRIDGE, SHOWING TUCKER IN THE PRISONER'S CAGE

Charles Tucker sits in the defendant's "cage," used in Massachusetts superior courthouses until the 1960s. Boston Globe, *courtesy of Newspapers.com.*

Other witnesses confirmed Tucker's accounts of his perambulations on the day of the murder, placing him no closer than Cutter's Corner. Tucker did not testify but did make a statement to the jury describing his movements on the day of the murder and explaining how he broke the knife out of fear after reporters and police became so interested in him. "I also wish to say, gentlemen, that on March 31 I was just as happy as any boy could be. I had everything in this world to live for, a good mother and father and a good home."

The case went to the jury on the afternoon of January 24. They returned that same night around 10:00 p.m. with a verdict of guilty in the first degree. Tucker was stunned and collapsed in a heap onto the rail of the prisoner's cage. He was sentenced to die in the electric chair at Charlestown State Prison.

James Vahey continued working tirelessly for his client, doing everything in his power to save the young man's life and taking no financial compensation for his efforts from the moment the verdict was announced. In April, he requested and was denied a new trial by the original trial judges Sherman and Sheldon. The Supreme Judicial Court of Massachusetts denied Tucker a new trial in October, overruling each of Vahey's eighteen defense exceptions to the trial court's ruling. Tucker's execution date was set for the second week of June 1906.

Less than a month before Tucker's scheduled execution date, the case took a page right out of a Perry Mason novel when a previously unknown man confessed to the murder. Jerry Hayes, also known as J. Moulton Hayes, was an itinerant laborer described as "a weak-faced man with weak and watery blue eyes of small caliber which are held apart by a long and bulbous nose" who looked "for all the world like a picture of the typical tramp from a comic paper" and "wore a suit that would not command an offer of 11 cents at Salem Street." Hayes had been in the Weston area around the time of the murder and eventually made his way to the small town of Bingham, Maine, where he worked on the railway and boarded at the home of Margaret Brown. According to Brown, Hayes confessed to her one morning in the fall of 1905 while she was sitting at the breakfast table reading the newspaper account of the crime. He claimed he had been passing by South Avenue in Weston looking for odd jobs and entered the house to ask for a drink of water. "Tucker got the chair, I tell you, and I would have got the chair if I hadn't got out of the house before the hue and cry arose," he told the stunned widow.

Although a year and a half had passed since the murder, and Charles Tucker had been convicted, Hayes's story was credible enough to prompt Brown to write to Tucker's mother, who passed on the information to her son's defense team. Sheriff Abram Page arrested Hayes on May 17 and placed him in jail in Skowhegan, Maine. When questioned further by the sheriff, Hayes admitted that he might have said such things to Brown while under the influence of alcohol, and any knowledge of the murder had come to him by reading the papers. Neither the prosecution nor the defense placed much stock in the drunken tale, and Hayes was released on May 19.

Undeterred, Vahey again filed a motion for a new trial based on new evidence concerning the Canadian stickpin and once again was denied. His final attempt at a new trial through the courts was the filing of a plea with the United States Supreme Court, claiming that Tucker's protection against illegal search and seizure under the Fourth Amendment was violated. This final plea was also unsuccessful.

After the highest court in the nation failed to save his client's life, Vahey took his case to the citizens of the commonwealth through a petition made available for signing at the offices of local newspapers across the state. Volunteers also went door-to-door to persuade residents to sign the petition;

one overzealous gentleman even had the audacity to visit the home of Edward Page, requesting his signature. (The seventy-nine-year-old died on April 6, 1906, following a period of rapidly declining health in the aftermath of his daughter's murder.)

In a little over six weeks, Vahey and associates managed to obtain the signatures of over 116,000 Massachusetts residents; among the signatories were bank presidents, school superintendents and religious and political leaders. According to Vahey, if joined together the petition would stretch out for more than a mile and "make a continuous line from the State House to the East Cambridge Jail." On May 22, the petition was packed into a large specially made wooden box, loaded on an express wagon and conveyed to the office of Governor Curtis Guild at the State House.

Tucker was transferred from the Middlesex County Jail in Cambridge to the "death house" at Charlestown State Prison on June 3. His fate now lay in the hands of the first-term governor; only a ruling of clemency by him could spare Tucker the chair. Governor Guild gave the matter serious consideration, reading the case files from all court proceedings, conferencing with Vahey and the defense team and even conducting his own investigation in which he revisited the crime scene, walking the neighborhood of the Page house and inserting the knife into the torn and bloody corset of Mabel Page. Guild concluded that the evidence overwhelmingly proved Tucker's guilt and on June 7 denied the plea. It was evident in the governor's statement that Tucker's character carried as much weight in his decision as the evidence. "Proof of the miserable habit of life of this unhappy young man as disclosed by incidents in connection with this trial is confirmed by my own independent investigation."

Other last-minute appeals came from sympathizers convinced of Tucker's innocence. Reverend Thomas Bishop had become Tucker's spiritual advisor and, after spending several hours speaking with him, appealed directly to the governor for clemency, without success. Bishop did manage to delay the execution by a day so that Tucker could be baptized. A group of Tucker's supporters telegrammed President Theodore Roosevelt, asking for his assistance in halting the execution. Roosevelt, who had known Guild since their college years at Harvard, sent him a telegram supporting the execution and affirming that it was a sound decision.

Vahey broke the news to Tucker that there would be no stay. He spent a long time with his client, taking care of some final requests, one of which was that the suit that Tucker had worn at trial be given to "some poor fellow who hasn't got a good suit." Shortly after midnight on June 12, Tucker walked unassisted to the death chamber. There would be no death house confession; Tucker proclaimed his innocence right to the end. He read a statement from a slip of paper he carried in his pocket: "I hope God will forgive me for all the wrongs I have done in my past life. I forgive everybody who has ever wronged me. I am at peace with my maker. May God have mercy on my soul." After a private funeral ceremony led by Reverend Bishop, Tucker was buried at Hope Cemetery, Worcester.

James Vahey was elected to the Massachusetts State Senate in 1906, representing the first Middlesex district. During his tenure in office, he worked to abolish the death penalty in Massachusetts. He also ran unsuccessfully for governor on the Democratic ticket three times from 1908 to 1910. He died in 1929 at just fifty-seven years of age.

Another sixty executions would take place before the last convicted murderer, Edward Gertsen, went to the chair in 1947. It wasn't until 1984 that the Supreme Judicial Court of Massachusetts abolished the death penalty.

7

NATICK AND MILFORD, 1923

THE *OTHER* MORSE FAMILY, PART 2

O n Monday evening, July 16, 1923, state police officer Carl L. Callahan heard noises in the bushes in the Pinewood Villa neighborhood, off Speen Street in West Natick. Emerging from them were Esther Morse, eighteen, and her apparent boyfriend, Alfred Augusto Machado, twenty-five. Morse conceded that while she had been meeting up with Machado regularly, she had done so out of fear. Machado said their meetings had been entirely consensual. Machado was placed under arrest and charged with assault and a statutory offense, as Morse was under the age of twenty-one.

Esther Morse lived with her mother, Lydia "Effie" (Towne) (Morse) Brummitt, in a modest house nearby at 23 Pinehurst Avenue. Her father, Frank Peabody Morse (1851–1910), was a second cousin of Mary Ann Morse, benefactress of the Morse Institute Library. (He was also a brother of the colorful Morse siblings we encountered in chapter 4.) Unlike them, he had married and moved out of the family house, albeit only around the block to Mill Street. There he operated a small farm that had been split off from his parents' much larger property. Not much is known about Frank, but in June 1910, he was arrested for attempted murder. The circumstances of his arrest are elusive, and Frank Morse died in the East Cambridge Jail in November 1910 while still awaiting trial. Effie was widowed with three children—fifteen-year-old Blanche, eleven-year-old Willard and six-year-old Esther. She sold the farm and remarried a widower named Horatio Brummitt, but that marriage evidently did not last. Blanche married at age twenty, while Willard got a job as a truck driver at a factory to support his mother and younger sister.

Esther had to report to court in Natick three days after the event to offer testimony against Machado at his arraignment. She was already in the courtroom on Thursday morning when Officer Callahan escorted Machado in. As soon as she saw them, she whipped out a small vial and drank a half-ounce of iodine, in an attempted suicide. The iodine left dark brownish stains on her lips and chin, which were noticed by the clerk of the court, Norman S. Trippe. Dr. William H. Cochran was called, identified the substance and had her taken to Leonard Morse Hospital in a taxicab. Machado's attorney told a reporter from the *Boston Globe* that his client had letters from Esther of an affectionate nature that he was prepared to offer into evidence and that Machado had proposed marriage. Machado was a native of Lousã, Portugal, who had arrived in New York in 1919 along with a brother. They immediately settled in Framingham, which already had a significant Portuguese community. (One cannot help but wonder whether an immigrant whose complexion was described as "dark" on his citizenship application was more likely to have been charged with an offense; on the other hand, they had been caught in flagrante delicto in the bushes off a public road.)

Esther was discharged from the hospital on Friday, and the court case was resumed a week later, on July 26. The state then made the surprise announcement that it was prepared to drop the case. Machado and Morse had gotten married by the clerk of Milford District Court on Saturday and were now husband and wife. Since a wife could not be compelled to testify against her husband, the prosecution had no recourse.

Apparently, it was indeed a love match, as they remained married until Machado's death in 1964. (How happy a union it proved is unknown. Machado, a junkman by trade, continued to appear in the police log for auto theft, bootlegging liquor during Prohibition, counterfeiting and, just a couple of years before his death, running numbers.) Esther Machado passed away in 1972.

Attempting suicide in a courtroom might seem a tad dramatic, but Esther was actually the more well-grounded of the two Morse sisters. Blanche had married at twenty and had four children in quick succession. Her husband, John Anderson, was a Swedish immigrant in poor health, so he was often out of work. They lived a hardscrabble existence in a tiny apartment in Natick. But for one glorious day, about six months before her sister's attempted suicide, Blanche (Morse) Anderson was the most glamorous woman in New England.

Blanche worked as a spiritualist on the side, casting horoscopes, reading palms, fortunetelling and the like. She endeavored to visit Alice H. Morgan, a noted clairvoyant, in Newtonville. Morgan catered to well-heeled clients, and Blanche might have wanted to learn how it was done. She couldn't afford her own reading, however, so when she visited Morgan, she had a plan. Calling at Morgan's house unannounced, Blanche acted surprised and asked if Morgan did not recognize her. When Morgan replied that she did not, Blanche announced that she was Anna Q. Nilsson, the Swedish-born silent film actress, one of the most popular stars of the day. Fortunately for Blanche, Alice Morgan had most definitely heard of Nilsson but was not familiar enough to realize she looked very little like her visitor. (A Swedish accent was easy for Blanche, of course. Since her husband was a Swedish immigrant, she knew enough of the language to fake it convincingly.) Morgan looked askance at Blanche's wardrobe, but the younger woman had an explanation. She needed to dress down to travel incognito, she confided. She was traveling to Boston, and Morgan's talents as a clairvoyant were so well-known that she had to pay a call. The flattered Morgan gave her a free reading, and the two women quickly became friends as "Anna Q. Nilsson" regaled her host with tales of Hollywood life. So much so that Morgan implored the actress to stay with her on her next trip to the area.

After about a week at home in Natick, Blanche hatched a plan. She went to Milford, where she placed an advertisement in the local weekly, announcing that Anna Q. Nilsson would be making an appearance the next day at the Milford Opera House to express her gratitude to the large Swedish American community in the area. The excited editor phoned Joseph Bernard Hurl, the theater's manager, who said that Nilsson's plans were news to him. Hurl rushed over to speak to Nilsson in person, and the bedraggled individual he encountered on that rainy January day certainly didn't look like a movie star. But as Hurl revealed later, he was in show business, so he knew that an actress's appearance on stage or screen was often artifice achieved with grease paint and lighting. Besides, Nilsson explained that her trunks had gone missing from her train and her maid was traveling the Eastern Seaboard in search of her wardrobe. Hurl implored Nilsson to delay her appearance for a few days so that he could book one of her films and properly promote the occasion. Blanche said that would be wonderful, and she could be reached at her good friend Alice Morgan's residence in Newtonville.

Morgan was delighted to see her new friend again and welcomed her to stay. She was sorry to hear about the loss of the movie star's luggage but told her that she could borrow some clothes until it arrived. When Hurl called to announce that he had booked Nilsson's film *What Women Will Do*

Blanche Morse Anderson, children at her feet, primping before a mirror before going out as Anna Q. Nilsson. San Francisco Examiner, *courtesy of Newspapers.com.*

and announced the star's appearance, Morgan sent Anna Q. Nilsson off to Milford in her best dress and a fur coat.

It might have been Alice Morgan's finest dress, but Joseph Hurl was not impressed when he met Blanche at the train station. It was a beautiful fur coat, but the dress was decidedly old fashioned. Hurl had an idea, though. "Still no sign of your luggage? Never mind! We'll go to the finest shops in Milford. Won't they be excited to loan their finest clothes and jewels to Anna Q. Nilsson!"

So it was that Anna Q. Nilsson was dressed to the nines, ready to introduce her greatest film in front of a sellout crowd of Swedish American fans at the Milford Opera House. The pit orchestra went into the Swedish national anthem as Nilsson walked from the wings. There she was met by Sallie Safstrom, chosen by the Milford Swedish Society, to present the star with a wreath of American Beauty roses. An account in the *San Francisco Examiner* relayed the spokeswoman's words: "Here are America's most beautiful roses for Sweden's most famous daughter." As the standing ovation started to fade away, a murmur began in the crowd. These were Nilsson's most ardent fans, after all, and they quickly began to question the identity of the woman on the stage. Hurl later said his suspicions began when he saw Blanche walk out before the footlights. An actress knows how to command a stage, and Blanche's walk was far too timid. Soon the hoots and cries of "Fake!" erupted across the auditorium. Nilsson asserted that they were making a huge mistake. She demanded to be taken to the police station, where she would prove her identity. Joseph Hurl stood on the stage and called on the audience to enjoy the film while he took Nilsson to sort it all out. The Milford Board of Selectmen, on hand for the proceedings, trailed along to the station as well.

Blanche was nothing if not a master storyteller, a quality she certainly shared with her aunt Electa. Her intimate knowledge of Hollywood gossip enthralled the group at the station house. A deciding factor seemed to be Blanche's knowing the precise dosage of morphine that had killed actor Wallace Reid earlier that month. The chief of police and selectmen decided that they had indeed made a terrible mistake and offered their own apologies before escorting her back to the theater, where the film was just ending. The police chief demanded the crowd offer the movie star their sincere apologies, and once again, the roar of applause filled the theater. Blanche was walking on air when she went to back to the depot to board the train back to Newtonville.

It was only a few days later, when the rapturous accounts of Anna Q. Nilsson's reception in Milford hit the national papers, that the Swedish

Blanche Morse Anderson, clutching her wreath of roses, being hooted offstage at the Milford Opera House. San Francisco Examiner, *courtesy of Newspapers.com.*

actress demanded to know who had been masquerading as her. Blanche Anderson was arrested for fraud, but she was such a good talker that she became a minor celebrity in her own right, and charges were dropped. Her profile ran coast to coast, and along with her well-documented turn as Nilsson, she told dubious tales of having infiltrated a stolen furs gang in Cochituate and an opium den in Boston's Chinatown. (Her story of posing as a female detective in a high-profile divorce case was verified, however, by her irate "client," Mrs. Thomas Pazolt of Boston.)

It was hard to go back to her dreary life in Natick, so she made plans to move to Framingham. She would establish a new life there and left her children with her mother while she got the new apartment ready. When John Anderson went to see the new apartment, he found it empty—Blanche had skipped town. It was only several months later, when Blanche read the account of her younger sister's attempted suicide in a Natick courtroom, that she finally returned home. She even served as Esther's maid of honor at her courthouse wedding to Alfred Machado in Milford, the scene of her recent triumph.

8

FRAMINGHAM, 1923

THE BODIES IN THE WOODS

T he first week of September 1923 had not been particularly hot or humid, yet for days the residents of Dennison Avenue had noticed a foul odor coming from the woods that bordered the eastern shore of Learned's Pond on the south side of town. The kettle pond had long been a popular swimming hole; trees lined most of the shoreline, with the exception of the southern shore where the Framingham Hospital stood. On the eastern shore, the forested patch known as Dennison Woods ran along the top of a hill and behind the backyards of the well-kept homes along Dennison Avenue. Both avenue and woods were named for the Dennison family, who had brought the paper and tag manufacturing company to Framingham from Roxbury in 1897. In 1923, it was one of the major employers in town.

Eventually, the odor in the woods became too much for residents to ignore, and on the afternoon of September 9, Charles Hall, his son Arthur and neighbor Raymond W. Boynton went searching for the source. It did not take them long to find it. Midway between the road and the pond, they discovered two bodies, apparently a man and a woman, although that was determined only by the clothing they were wearing, as decomposition was so advanced. The bodies were lying side by side with a revolver on the ground between them.

Soon after the discovery, Framingham police chief William Holbrook and medical examiner Dr. James Glass were at the scene, and despite the state of the bodies, Chief Holbrook was able to identify the pair based

Learned's Pond and Dennison Woods. *Courtesy of Framingham History Center.*

on a missing person report he had received over a week earlier. On September 1, forty-year-old Emidio Schiavi of nearby Clark Street had reported his wife, thirty-four-year-old Maria, missing. Emidio and Maria had arrived in America from the Abruzzo region of Italy as husband and wife in 1913 and, after living in Taunton for a few years, eventually settled in Framingham, where a large Italian immigrant population had been growing since the end of the nineteenth century. Emidio found work as a machinist at a rubber company near downtown Framingham. By 1923, the Schiavis had three young children, ages eight, six and four, but recently, there was tension in the house on Clark Street. Giuseppe (Joseph) Faba had known the family in Italy and had been boarding with them from the time they moved to Framingham. Recently, Emidio had noticed that Joseph was paying a little too much attention to Maria. On August 1, Emidio confronted Faba about his inappropriate attentions and demanded that he leave the house, which he did, moving to an apartment downtown. A few weeks after that, Faba was heard by his coworkers at the Dennison Manufacturing Company saying he was going to kill himself and "take someone with him." The comments were taken as a joke by those who heard them, until Faba disappeared at the beginning of September, the same time as Maria Schiavi.

The discovery of the pair did not clear up the entire mystery, and any narrative to match the gruesome scene in the woods could only be speculation. While police seemed inclined to believe the two met in the woods that day intent on carrying out a mutual suicide pact, family members described Maria as a loving mother who would never leave her children, either by eloping with another man or ending her own life. Faba's words to his Dennison coworkers and the three empty chambers in the gun would seem to corroborate the murder-suicide theory.

Fearful that his children might end up in an orphanage, Emidio Schiavi returned to Italy, where his relatives helped arrange a marriage for him. He returned to the United States the following June with his children and new wife, settling in Chester, Pennsylvania. He died in 1969 at the age of eighty-six.

9

MAYNARD, 1924

SLAIN BY A CORNCOB PIPE

On Saturday night, January 26, 1924, the party at 57 Butler Avenue in Maynard was beginning to get out of hand. A group of men had been drinking all night, and two of them had started to get into a violent argument. Their host feared the arrival of the police, and he would not have been charged with simply disturbing the peace. It was the height of Prohibition, and the possession of alcohol was illegal in the United States. So, he proceeded to kick the two adversaries, John Hankala and Werner Phillips, out into the frigid cold of a New England winter for them to continue their row elsewhere. (The high temperature in Boston that day had been a mere twenty-two degrees.)

Hankala and Phillips were actually close friends. Both natives of Finland (their pre-Anglicized names were Johan Hankala and Werner Matias Filppula, respectively), they worked together at the Assabet Mills of the American Woolen Company in Maynard. Hankala, at forty-eight, was eleven years older than Phillips. But he was also considerably larger, as he had been classified as both "tall" and "stout" on his draft card during the recent war, while Phillips had claimed to have been "physically unfit" for duty. They each had immigrated to America as young men, Hankala at twenty in 1896 and Phillips at thirteen in 1902.

Who or what had started the argument has been lost to time, but out on the street, the fight continued. Finally, having had enough, Hankala took a swing at the younger man. Unfortunately, he still had his corncob pipe in his hand, and it broke on impact with Phillips's face. Swearing up a storm, they

The house on Butler Avenue in Maynard, where John Hankala and Werner Phillips got into a fight that spilled out into the street, 2020. *Photo by author.*

each stumbled back to their separate homes and to their wives and children. When Phillips arrived at his home at 23 Glendale Street, his wife, Fannie, was shocked at the open wound beneath one of his eyes. She called a doctor to attend to her husband. He stitched up the large gash and departed.

By Sunday morning, Werner's pain was excruciating. Another doctor looked at it and advised him to take the train into Boston and see the specialists at the Massachusetts Eye and Ear Infirmary. Taking an X-ray, the doctors could see that part of the stem of Hankala's pipe had actually broken off and was lodged under his eye. The Maynard physician's stitches were removed, and surgeons extracted an approximately one-inch section of pipe stem made of bone from Phillips's eye socket.

While Werner Phillips languished in his hospital bed, John Hankala was arrested at his 13 Dartmouth Street home and charged with assault and battery. Released on bail, Hankala returned to work at the mill. The next Saturday, February 2, Phillips passed away in his hospital bed in Boston. John Connors, deputy chief of the Maynard Police Department, promptly re-arrested Hankala. On Monday, Hankala was arraigned on the charge of murder before Judge Prescott Keyes in Concord District Court. The newspapers reported that both the Hankala and Phillips families were devastated by the events. The families were respected, and this incident was viewed as quite uncharacteristic. The two men had been close friends, after all, and no one doubted that John Hankala had no intention of seriously injuring, let alone killing, Werner Phillips.

Hankala's trial was eventually set for April 30, 1924, but at this point, the case disappeared from the news. It seems likely a plea deal was reached. How much time, if any, Hankala served is unknown. But by 1928, Hankala was at home in Maynard for the marriage of his only surviving daughter, Hilja, to Albert O. Carlson. He continued working at the Assabet Mills at least through 1940, when he was sixty-five. His wife, Alma Naponen Hankala, passed away in 1944, and he died eleven years later, at the age of eighty, in 1955.

Meanwhile, the Phillips family's misfortunes continued. Fannie Carlson Phillips died on September 4, 1934, at the age of forty-one, as the result of injuries sustained in a fall. Werner and Fannie's son, Edwin R. Phillips, also a millworker, died in 1943 of tuberculosis at the age of thirty-one. Only their daughter, Gertrude Phillips Hendrickson, lived out a long life, passing away in California at the age of ninety in 2000.

10

SUDBURY, 1925

THE KLAN RIDES AGAIN

Most people associate the Ku Klux Klan with the South during Reconstruction, conjuring images of hooded figures on horseback riding in the night terrorizing freed Black people. But in the years following World War I, scenes of robed Klansmen riding in Model Ts past colonial town greens and gathering in fields surrounded by stone walls were becoming quite common in New England. The revival of the Klan began with the widespread popularity of D.W. Griffith's movie about the Reconstruction era, *The Birth of a Nation*, released in 1915. Whereas the earlier incarnation of the KKK had targeted formerly enslaved people, this new version rose up primarily in opposition to the large wave of Catholic and Jewish immigration that had taken place in the first two decades of the twentieth century and was largely centered not in the states that had joined the Confederacy but in the states that had remained loyal to the Union. Massachusetts was no exception. By 1925, the Roman Catholic Church had become the largest religious group in the United States, and for many, this represented a threat to their cultural traditions, economic power and religious views.

The year 1924 had seen an increase in Klan activity across the Bay State, and after a lull during the cold winter months, this activity picked up again in the spring and summer. Crosses were burned in Clinton and Winchendon. In Framingham, parishioners from both St. Bridget's Church in the center of town and St. George's in Saxonville witnessed cross burnings aimed at sending a message to their congregation. Outside of Worcester, where recent gatherings had numbered in the thousands, much of the Klan activity in the Commonwealth was occurring in the rural towns of Central Massachusetts and MetroWest. Each week, hundreds, sometimes thousands, of Klan members met in large fields to share their hateful rhetoric and misguided patriotism.

In May, police broke up a Klan meeting of three hundred in the Pinewood Villa section of Natick and arrested a Boston man just as he was about to set fire to a large cross. Two men were beaten in Northbridge at a gathering of over six hundred. In June, a crowd of ten thousand in Southwick listened to their leader, known only as the "Colonel," proclaim, "We may have to kill someone yet, but if we start I can tell you we have the numbers and the qualities to do it right."

None of these gatherings went unnoticed by the local citizens who were opposed to the Klan and its ideology. As word spread through towns about a Klan meeting, hundreds of opponents known as "antis" would arrive at the gathering to harass and jeer the members. Cars were vandalized, rocks were thrown and sometimes confrontations turned violent. One such riot took place in Upton when anti-Klansmen surrounded the meeting, threw stones and smashed the windshields of the participants. Similar incidents occurred in Milbury, Woburn, Leicester and Burlington.

On August 2, sleepy Westwood was the site of a battle between Klansmen and opponents that would take police from four towns and the state patrol to control. For weeks, Stephen Illsley, although advised against it by local police, had been distributing flyers advertising a Klan gathering in the field behind his farmhouse on Washington Street in the Islington section of town (near present-day St. Denis Church). Illsley claimed that he was hosting the event solely to make a profit from the sale of sandwiches and tonic (soft drinks) and was not actually a member of the Klan himself.

The melee started just moments after the first speaker, Miss Jessie Sawyer, began to address the crowd. A rock was hurled by one of the protestors, who soon overran the field and the wooden bleachers that had been set up. Fights between the two groups erupted, punches were thrown and clubs swung through the air. The crowd surged onto the property, ripping the hoods and robes from the perimeter guards and beating them. The Klan retreated into the house. The mob then stormed the speakers' area, with some members doing an impromptu show featuring dancing and singing before destroying the stage. The Klan members remained besieged in the house for some time while Westwood police attempted to disperse the crowd. Every window in the Illsley house was smashed by rocks, and many of the furnishings were damaged. Order was finally restored around 7:30 p.m., when officers from Dedham, Needham, Norwood and the state police barracks in Framingham arrived, but even with their arrival, the confrontation continued. Klansmen were assaulted as they ran to their cars, some of them having their Klan robes snatched from them by exuberant youth.

Two men, Perley Libbey and Leroy Hall, both of Sudbury, were arrested and charged with possession of a concealed weapon when their car was pulled over in Dedham and a revolver was found hidden in the back seat. Hall just happened to be the son of Sudbury police chief Seneca Wilson "Sen" Hall. Neither of the men was deterred by this setback, for the following week, they were both at the center of the violence that would erupt in their hometown.

Perley W. Libbey was a forty-three-year-old husband and father of two who had come to Sudbury from Boston some time before 1917. He lived with his family on a farm on Landham Road, just over the town line from the Saxonville section of Framingham. Libbey had been hosting weekly Klan meetings on his property all summer, and after posting bond on his weapons charge, he quickly made plans for another gathering on August 10. After the experience in Westwood, he wisely went to the state police headquarters in Framingham to inform them of the meeting and warn that there might be some trouble. Sudbury selectman Charles Way had also warned of potential trouble at the Libbey farm

Chief Hall and several Sudbury officers were the only police on hand as darkness fell over the Libbey farm. About one hundred Klansmen had arrived by 9:30 p.m. As the meeting progressed, twice as many antis had gotten the word and filled the road in front of the Libbey farmhouse, jeering and chanting and waiting for the meeting to end. There are conflicting accounts of the number of Klansmen and protestors gathered that night, and both sides were quick to lay the blame on the other. It is safe to say that after their experience in Westwood the week before, the Klan was not about to be trapped inside a house by an angry mob for a second time. At some point, the Klansmen spread out across the property to make a stand, hiding behind outbuildings, shrubs and stone walls. The usual shouting and stone throwing by the anti-Klansmen commenced, but suddenly, gunfire erupted from behind a henhouse, and five of the spectators fell wounded. The wounded men were quickly packed into autos and rushed to the home of Dr. Christopher Carr in Saxonville. The majority of the wounds were superficial, but if the weapons fired had been loaded with anything more

Framingham police chief William W. Holbrook. *Courtesy of Framingham History Center.*

powerful than buckshot there certainly would have been dead bodies lying in the road. One victim, twenty-three-year-old Alonzo Foley of Saxonville, was so severely wounded that Father John McCauley of St. George's Church was summoned to the scene to administer last rites. Foley eventually recovered under the expert care of noted neurosurgeon Dr. Harvey Cushing.

Back at the Libbey farmhouse, state police, led by Lieutenant Charles Beaupre, arrived on motorcycles to help the beleaguered and outmanned Sudbury force. Assisted by the Framingham and Sudbury forces, Beaupre and his men cordoned off the area and began a search of the property for those Klansmen who had not managed to escape. Many of them, including Chief Hall's son Leroy, had to be rooted out from hiding spots in barns, under bushes and behind sheds. In all, over seventy-five were arrested and taken to the police station in downtown Framingham. Chief William Holbrook had a difficult time squeezing them all into the small building, and by night's end, all but fifteen had been released. A cache of weapons seized at the farm included several rifles, ammunition belts, bullets and cudgels.

The fifteen Klansmen appeared before Judge Edward W. Blodgett in Framingham the following day, charged with assault with a dangerous weapon. The men were from Sudbury, Maynard, Stow, Needham, Wellesley, Newton and North Easton. The Klansmen were represented by Nils T. Kjellstrom and J. Walton Tuttle, who arranged for bail of $200 each and a continuance of the case until August 19. The case was eventually dropped by the state for insufficient evidence, and all the defendants were free to go.

On August 12, Perley Libby and Leroy Hall were found guilty of the gun charges they faced from the Klan rally in Westwood and were each sentenced to a year in the Dedham House of Correction. After appealing their conviction in superior court, the pair had a jury trial in Dedham on September 23 and were found not guilty.

Klan gatherings continued across the state throughout the summer of 1925, but the KKK's presence in Massachusetts was ebbing, due in large part to the active opposition from local citizens. Each Klan event was met with protests, often violent, often led by groups of Catholics of various ethnicities. By 1930, Klan membership in the state had dropped below one thousand from a high of more than ten thousand just a few years earlier and soon faded away entirely.

11

CONCORD AND FRAMINGHAM, 1928

HEADLINER-THE FREDERICK HINMAN KNOWLTON STORY

Before he had even reached the age of twenty-five, Hinman Knowlton had had enough notoriety to last anyone a lifetime. As a young man, he had been at the center of several dramatic and newsworthy events. As it turns out, these events were mere prelude to the ultimate drama that would play out in the spring and summer of 1928.

Frederick Hinman Knowlton went by his middle name to avoid being confused with his father, Frederick Harold Knowlton, a Framingham selectman and president of the Framingham Business College. The first of Hinman's headline-grabbing feats occurred in July 1909, just before the seventeen-year-old was to begin his sophomore year at Framingham Academy. While waiting at a dock for his parents to return from a boating trip on Learned's Pond, Hinman heard calls for help coming from the deeper water of the pond. He saw two young women struggling in the water and immediately threw off his shoes and jumped in to their rescue. An expert swimmer, the teen swam out and pulled the panicked and thrashing girls to safety. By the time he got the victims to shore, they had passed out and were only brought back to consciousness by staff members from nearby Framingham Hospital, where they both worked as nurses. The *Boston Globe* ran a story on the near tragedy, with an accompanying photograph of the young hero and his faithful dog beside him. On November 30, the Massachusetts Humane Society awarded Knowlton a silver medal for his bravery.

Just days later, Knowlton again made headlines across the country in a bizarre and mysterious incident that occurred at the family's home on Henry Street. In the early dawn hours of December 2, Dr. Ezra Hobbs was called to the Knowlton home, where he found Mr. Knowlton bleeding heavily from the mouth and his wife, Hinman's stepmother, Harriet, in hysterics. Also crowding the apartment were several neighbors and young Hinman, who was in a highly agitated state. Dr. Hobbs quickly assessed the situation; Mr. Knowlton had been shot by a small caliber pistol, and the bullet had lodged in his jaw after breaking off two of his teeth. Although it appeared that Mrs. Knowlton had also been grazed by a bullet, later examination showed that she had only suffered cuts caused by some unknown source. Dr. Hobbs removed the bullet right there in the Knowlton home and, after some interrogation on his part, learned what little there was to know about the confusing scene.

At around 6:00 a.m., Mr. and Mrs. Knowlton, who lived on the first floor, as well as Arline Chandler and her father, Edward, who lived above them, were awakened by the sound of shots being fired. Another neighbor who lived next door, Brainard Rice, was also awakened and came to the Knowltons' door as soon as he could rouse himself. He then ran upstairs to the third floor, where he found Hinman sleeping so soundly that he had to be shaken by Rice to wake up.

There was no mystery concerning the gun that had fired the shots—it was lying right there on the floor of the Knowltons' bedroom and would later be identified as the gun that Hinman had purchased the previous Fourth of July to celebrate the holiday.

With no signs of a break-in at the scene, and Hinman's own gun lying on the floor of the bedroom, it was evident that the shooter had to have been a member of the household, but which one? There was no reason to suspect the Chandlers. And even if any of the Knowltons had the opportunity, they all readily admitted that there was no animosity or unpleasantness in the family that would have provoked such a potentially deadly attack.

Faced with these uncertainties, Mr. Knowlton offered an explanation that, although improbable, was the best that anyone could come up with. In the past, Hinman had occasionally been seen walking in his sleep. Perhaps, suggested Mr. Knowlton, the boy had accidentally shot his parents while sleepwalking. This theory of Mr. Knowlton's caused the story to "go viral" by 1909 standards. The next day, newspapers across the country featured headlines such as "Sleepwalker Is Held for Reckless Shots" (Billings, Montana), "Boy Asleep Shoots Father" (Sheboygan, Wisconsin) and "Mysterious Attacks Due to Sleepwalker?" (Fort Worth, Texas).

With no clear picture of what happened in the apartment on Henry Street, Framingham police took no immediate action on the matter.

However, around 4:00 p.m., Framingham patrolman Walter F. Taylor arrived at the Knowlton home with an arrest warrant for the suspect—the hero of Learned's Pond, young Hinman Knowlton himself. The arrest came after a long telephone call between police and Abner Gould Whittaker, the father of Hinman's stepmother. In a long conversation with the chief, Whittaker described Hinman as unstable and possibly insane. He told of an incident several years previously in which Hinman went missing from the family home after an altercation with his father and eventually returned after spending several days with relatives in Worcester. Whittaker also reported that Hinman had recently purchased new clothing and other items with no apparent source of income.

Willis Kingsbury sat on the bench of the First District Court of Southern Middlesex County from 1886 to 1920. *Courtesy of Framingham History Center.*

The following day, Knowlton was arraigned in Framingham District Court before Judge Willis Kingsbury (the same judge who had presided over the Andrew Emery/Nina Danforth inquest some seven years earlier). Hinman was released on $500 bail and ordered to appear before the judge on December 11.

Mr. and Mrs. Knowlton defended their son, assuring interviewers that there was no animosity between father and son, and stuck with the sleepwalking narrative as the only possible explanation for the mystery. They hired John M. Merriam, a well-known and distinguished member of the community, to represent Hinman.

At the hearing, the prosecution contended that Hinman was the shooter. Merriam agreed that the shooting had indeed been done by a sleepwalker, but the identity of that somnambulist was not young Hinman but his father, Frederick. Mr. Knowlton's aunt Mary Bullard was called as a witness to testify that the older man had been sleepwalking since his youth and had done many strange things in his sleep. Also testifying was Dr. George Adams, superintendent of Westborough State Hospital. Dr. Adams confirmed that it was indeed possible for a person to have done such an act in his sleep. He had examined Hinman and found "no tendencies of a homicidal character."

Photo by Hudson.
JOHN M. MERRIAM,

John M. Merriam was a respected Framingham lawyer and selectman who defended Hinman Knowlton on charges that he shot his father. *Courtesy of Framingham History Center.*

According to Merriam, the night before the shooting, there had been a family discussion about the gun that Hinman had purchased the previous July. Mrs. Knowlton was very nervous about keeping a loaded revolver in the house. At the end of the discussion, Mr. Knowlton locked it in the drawer of a desk in Hinman's room on the third floor.

Merriam contended that Mr. Knowlton, extremely worried and unsettled about the gun situation, got out of bed while still sleeping, climbed the stairs to the third floor and retrieved the gun. He then walked back down to his bedroom, and while attempting to unload the gun, it went off, firing three shots, including the one that entered his own mouth, nearly killing him. Judge Kingsbury found insufficient evidence of Hinman's guilt and declared him not guilty.

Eight years later, the now twenty-three-year-old Hinman was once again in the news, at the center of yet another mysterious incident. In late June 1917, Hinman was reported missing from the Framingham home he shared with his wife of one year, Gladys Bragg. Witnesses told Framingham police they had seen the young man in Worcester, withdrawing money from several banks and purchasing a suit in the city. Later, that suit was found folded neatly by the shores of Lake Quinsigamond, giving the impression that Knowlton had drowned in the lake either intentionally or by accident. The disappearance was cleared up somewhat when Knowlton showed up at Fort Slocum in New York after enlisting in the army as a radio engineer. He served in that role in Texas and was discharged in 1918, whereupon he returned to Framingham.

Knowlton passed the next few years quietly, staying out of the headlines and working as an instructor at his father's Framingham Business College. He eventually opened his own automobile and battery shop on Irving Street in Framingham, and in 1923, he and Gladys welcomed a new son.

On the night of Friday, March 30, 1928, while motoring along the desolate Concord Turnpike about a mile from the historic town's center, salesman Willis F. Bird made a startling and disturbing discovery. On the side of the

Marguerite Stewart's body was found along this lonely stretch of the Concord Turnpike, which has changed very little over the years. *Photo by author.*

road by a section of fence railing spanning a small brook was the body of a woman. It appeared to Bird that the woman had been hit by a car, but when police arrived and examined the body, they realized quickly that she had been the victim of foul play, having suffered a vicious blow to the back of the head from a blunt object. The lack of blood at the scene indicated that she had been killed elsewhere and her body left at this remote location. She carried no identification, but a handkerchief embroidered with the name "M. Stewart" was found in her pocket, offering a vital clue to her identity. She was well-dressed and appeared to be in her late twenties.

Within hours of the first newspaper reports of the discovery, the young woman was identified as twenty-eight-year-old Marguerite Stewart, a supervisor at the Beverly School for the Deaf. School officials had reported her missing on Friday night around 6:00 when she failed to show up for work after her day off on Thursday. Stewart's brother Wallace identified the body and several personal articles found at the scene, including a photograph of ten-year-old Jeannette Stewart, who was a student at the school for the deaf and the daughter of Marguerite.

State police continued to scour the Concord site for clues while detectives traveled to Beverly to interview school officials and to Worcester to gather information from Stewart's father, Charles. In Worcester, the grieving Mr. Stewart provided a short list of men who were known acquaintances of his daughter. At the Beverly School, detectives checked phone records for calls Marguerite might have made or received and spoke with staff members who had been the last to see her. Both avenues of investigation led to one primary suspect in the brutal crime.

On Wednesday, while Marguerite's family gathered by her grave in Concord's famous Sleepy Hollow Cemetery, state police detectives were at the East Cambridge police station conducting what would turn out to be a fourteen-hour interview with their chief suspect, the hero of Learned's Pond, Frederick Hinman Knowlton of Framingham.

During the questioning, Knowlton at first denied knowing Marguerite Stewart but later confessed they had met about eight years previously when she was a student at the Framingham Business College and he an instructor. He then revealed they had kept up their acquaintanceship over the years. He also admitted that he had been with Stewart on Thursday, the day before her body was found. According to Knowlton, he had spent the day with her but had dropped her off near the entrance to the school at 10:30 p.m.

Knowlton's statements concerning the nature of his relationship with Stewart were contradictory. At first, he insisted they were merely friends, then he broke down in tears and admitted they were in love and then finally he went back to his original story that it was just a friendship. What he couldn't explain was why on Saturday, the day after the body was discovered, he made some repairs to his car and washed it with chloride of lime. His actions did not reflect those of an innocent man. The police thought so, too, and on April 5, he was arrested and charged with murder.

The trial began on June 4, 1928, in the East Cambridge courthouse. The prosecution team believed they had a strong case against Knowlton, despite the fact that the location of the murder was never determined, and no murder weapon was found. They contended that, although married, Knowlton had carried on an illicit relationship with Marguerite Stewart for many years, meeting her regularly. He was the last person seen with her alive when he picked her up at the Beverly School on Thursday morning, March 29. An eyewitness described seeing a man who could have been Knowlton sitting with a weeping woman in Weston in a car that fit the description of Knowlton's just three hours before the body was found. Knowlton's actions in the days following the murder were certainly the actions of a man who

The sign for the Framingham Business College can be seen in the upper windows of this business block in downtown Framingham. *Courtesy of Framingham History Center.*

had something to hide. He painted his car and washed it with a bleach solution, although that did little to hide the blood found in the rumble seat.

Knowlton took the stand in his own defense and tried to explain both his relationship with the deceased and his suspicious behavior in the days following her death. He claimed that he had never had a romantic relationship with Stewart. They were very close friends and she often called on him for advice, as she had on March 29. He insisted that he last saw her at 10:30 p.m. the night of the twenty-ninth when he dropped her off in Beverly. At the presumed time of the murder, around 7:00 p.m. on Friday the thirtieth, Knowlton claimed he was in Sherborn collecting a bill from a customer (the customer in question, a Mr. Johnson, testified he never saw Knowlton on that day). According to Knowlton, the blood found in the back of his car belonged to his wife, who suffered an accident several days before the murder. He explained that he washed the car with a bleach solution to remove battery acid that had spilled during a delivery run.

The jury began deliberating on June 13 and returned just five hours later with a guilty verdict. In December, Knowlton's attorneys appealed to the Supreme Judicial Court, but the plea was denied. Sentencing was delayed when a new witness came forward claiming she had seen Stewart in Worcester on the day she was murdered, being driven in a car by a man who was not Knowlton. Investigators found no merit in this claim, and on March 9, 1929, Knowlton was sentenced to die in the electric chair the week of May 12. The expected appeal for clemency was denied by Governor Frank Allen on May 8, and the execution date was set for shortly after midnight on May 13.

Knowlton's wife, Gladys, who had remained mostly in the background throughout the trial, made a direct appeal to the governor, with no success. She and Knowlton's sister were the last to visit him the day before his execution. Shortly after midnight on May 13, Knowlton was playing a game of cribbage with several guards who had befriended him when officials came to escort him to the death chamber. He walked calmly to the chair, offered no last words and was pronounced dead at eleven minutes past midnight. Two days earlier, a poem written by Knowlton, titled "Life's Condiment," appeared in the *Boston Globe*. The final stanza read:

> *For every ray of sunshine there is a drop of rain*
> *In every breath of gladness*
> *There is a twinge of pain*
> *The beauties of a garden*
> *Are sullied by the weeds*
> *The happiness of humans*
> *Is marred by unkind deeds.*

The final headline for this young man who had been making news since his boyhood appeared on page one of the *Globe* on May 14, 1929. It read simply: "Knowlton Calmly Dies in the Chair."

12

STOW, 1930

THE POLISH FARMHOUSE MURDER

He said his name was Charles Calahot, but everyone just called him Charlie George. He came into the lawyer's office that day in early August 1930 because he wanted to get paid. He had worked as a hired hand out in Stow on the old George Hale farm since June and had yet to see a dime, and neither had his buddy John Stavis. Whenever they asked the man who hired them, Joe Stefanoski, he would say he was merely the manager. They really needed to talk to the farm owner, but he was away with no definite date for his return. Charlie George had never met anyone at the farm except Joe, and all he knew was that times were tough, farm work was hard and *somebody* owed him his wages. The occasional "party" Stefanoski would throw for his farmhands was not enough.

The lawyer started to make some inquiries around town. He quickly discovered that there were a number of complaints about the management of the George Hale farm. The farm had been owned since 1927 by a Polish couple, Wincenty "William" and Stanislawa "Stacia" Stefanowicz, but no one had seen them since May. The foreman, Joe Stefanoski, seemed to be running things, but bills were going unpaid. When Joe bought grain for the farm from J.J. Cushing in Hudson in June, he had signed the receipt "Stefanowicz" and charged it to the farm. When he sold milk from the farm to the Whiting Company in Boston or collected rent on the couple's other farm in West Concord, however, Stefanoski had pocketed the money directly. Calahot's attorney checked with the Middlesex Registry of Deeds and determined that the Stefanowiczes still owned the farm. Things were not adding up. Nonetheless, the lawyers drafted a bill of attachment on the farm for the workers' lost wages. Middlesex County sheriff John R. Fairbairn went to the farm on Tuesday, August 5, 1930, to give notice of the attachment. (You will recall that Fairbairn, now seventy-nine years old, had held both Nina Danforth and Charles Tucker in custody. He would serve thirty-four years as sheriff, until his death at the age of eighty-two in 1933.) Stefanoski was nowhere to be found, so the sheriff officially placed Charlie George Calahot in charge of the farm.

Meanwhile, members of Stefanowicz's family were growing worried. The couple had no children, but they had a niece, Anna (Bobnis) Skirton, who lived nearby in Maynard. Anna had been out to the farm in late May and asked Joe Stefanoski about the whereabouts of her aunt and uncle. Stefanoski told her that William had been having stomach trouble, and they had both gone to Chicago so that he could be operated on by a famous Polish surgeon. Suspicious, Anna asked him more detailed questions, and he insisted they had taken a big trunk of clothes with them so would

The old George Hale farmhouse in Stow, home of the Stefanowiczes, 2020. *Photo by author.*

probably be gone a while. Sometime later, she returned to the farmhouse with her husband, Vincent Skirton, while Stefanoski was away. After looking around, they found the Stefanowiczes' steamer trunk in another room in the house, which confirmed to them that the farmhand had been lying. On Wednesday, August 6, the day after the sheriff served the attachment, the Skirtons convinced the local undertaker in Maynard, Warren A. Twombly, to travel out to Stow with them. Stefanoski was still absent, so they made a thorough inspection of the house. In the Stefanowiczes' bedroom, their bed was missing, but the bed linens were piled in a corner, along with some clothing that belonged to the couple. There were other clothes hanging from nails in the closet and a bureau with its drawers half open that contained "a handful of papers and letters." On the floor were suspicious-looking stains, fifteen in all, that Twombly determined could have been blood. Twombly decided it was time to alert the state police.

State police detectives were soon able to determine that the last confirmed sighting of the Stefanowiczes was at the offices of Dr. John Middleton on May 21, 1930. William Stefanowicz had indeed been suffering minor stomach trouble, but Dr. Middleton assured police that he had been treated successfully and certainly had not required any surgery. That meant that the couple had been missing for ten full weeks before the police were called. In retrospect, probably the main reason for that delay was the couple's isolation. First, there was the remote setting of the farm itself, with few neighbors and lacking even a telephone. The Stefanowiczes were also socially isolated, having no children, and as Polish immigrants in an almost entirely Yankee rural town. True, there was a large Polish community in neighboring Hudson, but the demands of running a farm meant the Stefanowiczes mostly kept to themselves.

Once the investigation finally started, it proceeded rapidly. On Thursday, August 7, Corporal Raymond Foley took charge of the potential scene of the crime—the Stefanowicz farm—while state police detectives Edward P. O'Neill and Edward J. Sherlock began interviewing possible witnesses. The Stefanowiczes' nearest neighbor was eighty-five-year-old George Washington Warren Edson. In addition to being a farmer, he was a Civil War veteran, had once studied law, was briefly a toy manufacturer and had long been a draughtsman for a foundry in Hudson. He was perhaps best known in town as a singer, photographer and poet. He was so devoted a poet, in fact, that in 1910 he ran for the state legislature, campaigning entirely in verse. Perhaps even more remarkably, he won, becoming the first Democrat to represent Stow in over fifty years. In 1922, at the age of seventy-six, he decided he should settle down and got married to Clare MacKay, a woman twenty-six years his junior. Clare was about the same age as her neighbor, Stacia Stefanowicz, and she befriended the lonely Polish farm wife. "Mrs. Stevens," as Clare called her, "because it was easier to pronounce," greatly missed her former home in West Concord—their neighbors, electricity, running water, telephone and the relative bustle of village life. Clare assured the officers that Mrs. Stevens "hated that farmhouse and everything about it so bitterly that she would have told everybody on earth if she had been planning to go away for such a long time!"

Clare had always assumed that farmhand Joe Stefanoski must have been a relative, his name being so similar to Stefanowicz. (Police did not record if Clare called him "Mr. Stevens" as well.) But she had heard from Mrs. Stevens that Joe resented the amount of work he was required to do on account of his employer's age and that he was prone to rage, especially after drinking. On one occasion, the farmhand had even smashed Mrs. Stevens's cast-iron kitchen stove.

Another neighbor, seventy-nine-year-old Charles Yapp, had gone to the Stefanowicz farm in June to see about money he was owed for hay. Joe Stefanoski told him the same story he had told Anna Skirton, that William Stefanowicz had gone with his wife to Chicago for an operation. This time he added a further detail, that Stefanowicz had probably died, but in any case, had deeded the farm over to him before he left. Stefanoski did pay Yapp later in June, after he sold off the farm's twenty-two head of cattle, but Yapp admitted he still found the story a little odd.

Hudson's chief of police, Andrew Megarty, began interviewing members of Hudson's Polish community. He learned Stefanoski had been in town a few days earlier but had since disappeared. Police also sought to speak to Stefanoski's thirty-year-old Polish girlfriend, whom, he had told the other farmhands, would soon marry him and live on the farm once she had finished serving time in New Hampshire for bootlegging.

In the meantime, police determined that it was time to comb the farm for the bodies of the Stefanowiczes. This was no small task, as the property encompassed some 176 acres, including a cedar swamp that the locals claimed was surrounded by quicksand and a pond said to be bottomless. (Much of this area is now encompassed in the town's Hale Corzine conservation land.) An initial search of a recently excavated area turned up skeletons of a horse, a cow and a dog, but no human remains. Police probed the hay bales in the barn with their prodding irons but still turned up nothing. It was decided to assemble a large number of local and state police officers, along with volunteers, to conduct a more comprehensive search beginning the next day, Friday, August 8, headed by state police corporal Foley.

That weekend, a spectacle hitherto unknown in Stow occurred when a crowd numbering in the hundreds (with some estimates over one thousand) gathered near the farmhouse at the corner of Hudson and Athens Roads. So many automobiles jammed the narrow country lanes that the Stow chief of police, Peter Larson, ordered his men pulled off the search detail to direct traffic and maintain some sense of order in the carnival-like atmosphere. Other officers were charged with keeping the crowds out of the house itself, so eager were people for a look around inside. In the end, the police were so overwhelmed that the crowds roamed freely through the meadows, pine groves and even Joe Stefanoski's vegetable garden, conducting their own searches up and down Athens Road. Photographers from the major Boston dailies were on the farm as well. With little to cover, they passed the time photographing the crowds as well as local police chiefs and other officials posing in front the house and various outbuildings. The only solid evidence turned up the first day was discovery of a half-buried mattress that was believed to have been from the Stefanowiczes' missing bed.

On Saturday, state police turned up a vital piece of evidence—not from the property but from the crowd of onlookers. Mrs. Delcia Bowser of Hudson had pushed her way to the front of the line and showed detective Sherlock something of great interest—a photograph she had taken of Joe Stefanoski three weeks earlier. Bowser had visited the farm on a berry picking expedition in late June and then returned twice more with friends. Stefanoski had even inquired whether she would be interested in becoming the housekeeper at the farm. State police took possession of the photo and the negative.

Late on Sunday afternoon, the fourth full day of searching, police had begun to despair of ever turning up the Stefanowiczes. Then at 3:43 p.m., fifteen-year-old George Estabrook of Hudson came running down the hill to the house yelling that he and some other boys had found something. Warren Twombly, the Maynard undertaker who had first found the traces of blood in the bedroom, and Corporal Foley followed Estabrook up the lane. Just behind them was a vast crowd of onlookers who were stirred into action by the news that some boys had finally found something. This strange procession left the lane through a meadow and then went into the woods on a path that crossed a mostly dry stream bed and headed uphill. There, off the path, they spotted the other three boys—Charles Leonard, nineteen, of Hudson, as well as Emerson Chickering, seventeen, and Hobart King, fifteen, both of West Acton. Next to them was something sticking out of the ground. As Twombly approached, he recognized the object as a human elbow and turned to Foley, "This is it! This is the place." Word was sent to the state police that detectives O'Neill and Sherlock needed to return to the farm at once. Meanwhile, Charlie George Calahot, the laborer whose desire to be paid for his work had started the whole inquiry, was sent to fetch the farm wagon to transport the bodies back down to the house once they had been excavated from their shallow grave.

At the house, Dr. Clyde H. Merrill, associate medical examiner, looked over the bodies. Both heads were crushed, presumably by an axe. Mrs. Stefanowicz was killed by a blow to the left side of the head and another across her face. She was buried in her clothes—a long skirt, woolen shawl and house cap. Mr. Stefanowicz was killed by blows to the back of the head and across his face and nose. He was also buried fully clothed in his farm overalls and heavy shoes. His brown felt hat had a clean cut across it from where the axe blow had fallen. The bodies were then removed to Twombly's undertaking rooms in Maynard, where relatives identified that these were indeed the Stefanowiczes. (Charlie George and John Stavis, the two farmhands, suddenly realized there was indeed a murderer on the loose. They decided they would no longer stay in the farmhouse and erected a hut in the woods—oddly, quite near where the bodies had been exhumed earlier in the day.)

After the discovery of the bodies, the focus of the case shifted to the apprehension of Stefanoski. Police were following several leads—he was in Salem or Nashua, New Hampshire, looking to free his girlfriend. Another report had him in Concord, New Hampshire, a report deemed credible enough that Detective O'Neill took a train to investigate. Yet another had him staying with a relative in Malden, Massachusetts. No reports had him in Boston, and yet that is where Stefanoski was apprehended two days later in a hardware store on Stuart Street. He was recognized by a quick-thinking clerk, Harry A. Levy, who had left Stefanoski looking over catalogues of farming equipment while he ducked out back to phone the police. (It was later revealed that he had, in fact, spent two nights in Malden.)

When interrogated by Detectives O'Neill and Sherlock, Stefanoski at first stuck to the story that the Stefanowiczes had traveled to Chicago for surgery, and he claimed that he had even received a letter from them and written back. This was quickly disproved when it was determined that Stefanoski was illiterate in Polish as well as English. Stefanoski then said he had in fact witnessed the murder, only it was done by one of the other farmhands, John Stavis. It had taken place on the lane not far from where they were buried. First William Stefanowicz was beaten to death, and then Stacia, hearing the screams from the house, ran up to find her husband lying on the ground. When Stacia knelt over her husband's lifeless body, the killer had attacked again.

When the detectives cross-examined Stefanoski, he came to finally admit that it was he who had killed the Stefanowiczes in the lane leading to the cedar swamp. This seemed to wrap up the case nicely, except certain details Stefanoski told them were contradicted by the evidence. First, he said the murder weapon was a birch club, when William's hat was found with a big cut in it as if from an axe. Second, he said both murders happened in the lane behind the house, in which case, why were there stains in the bedroom and why had their mattress been buried on the property? Third, Stefanoski said he killed William Stefanowicz in a rage after being told that Charlie George would be running the farm, when from all other accounts, Charlie George and John Stavis had been hired by Stefanoski after the Stefanowiczes' disappearance. Finally, he stated that the murder happened on June 1, which was a full ten days after the couple had last been seen.

The confession lasted until well into the night. It was only the next morning that Stefanoski was assigned a court-appointed attorney for his arraignment. Ultimately, the prosecution, in the person of Middlesex district attorney Warren L. Bishop, largely went along with the version of events as relayed by Stefanoski in his confession, although they fixed the date of the murder as May 25.

Between the arraignment and the trial, prosecutors had learned that Stefanoski was an alias. When he lived in Portsmouth, New Hampshire, in the early 1920s, he had gone by the surname Groboski, but that was not his real name, either. Police learned his true identity, Joseph Belenski, when his wife, whom he had abandoned in Lynn with two children a decade before, came to the East Cambridge jail where he was being held. She shouted at him in Polish, "You devil." Stefanoski/Groboski/Belenski initially flinched at her appearance but then immediately settled back into the impassive demeanor he had shown throughout the entire ordeal.

The trial took place in November. Assistant District Attorney Frederick Crafts handled the case for the prosecution. John F. Daly, Belenski's attorney, was well-respected in the Cambridge courts and was not above a little showmanship. In 1925, he had made the front page of the *Boston Globe* after defending a man charged with non-support of his wife. After he had lost the case, he collected his fee from the defendant and then strolled to the other side of the courtroom and handed it to the plaintiff, his client's aggrieved wife.

Daly's principal tactic was to seek to get Belenski's confession ruled inadmissible, and he made several motions to that effect, all of which were rejected by Judge John H. Hammond. As a desperate attempt to spare his client's life, Daly put Belenski on the stand. Belenski testified that on June 9, he had been milking the cows in the barn when he heard Mrs. Stefanowicz cry out his name from the kitchen. Rushing into the house, he saw her prostrate on the floor in a pool of blood, William Stefanowicz standing over her with an iron hammer. He quickly ran to the well to get water to minister to his stricken mistress, but when he returned, William was wielding a shotgun and threatened to kill him as well. A fight ensued. The shotgun discharged but missed Belenski, and William was killed in the struggle. Belenski then hauled both bodies up the hill in a tip cart and buried them in the shallow grave where they were found. When asked why he did not notify the authorities, Daly suggested that his client "was not an intelligent man."

Closing arguments wrapped up by 11:15 a.m. on November 26, 1930. The court adjourned an hour for lunch, and then the jury began its deliberations. The jury reached a verdict less than three hours later. At 3:43 p.m., Judge Hammond read the verdict to the court—guilty on both counts. For once, Belenski looked shaken as the court translator rendered the verdict in Polish. Belenski asked, "Electric chair?" The translator nodded. Daly vowed to appeal, but this represented his second loss to the district attorney's office in less than a month. A few weeks earlier, as the Democratic candidate for Middlesex district attorney, Daly had lost to Craft's boss, Republican Warren L. Bishop, by a margin in excess of thirty thousand votes.

Daly appealed Belenski's case all the way to the Massachusetts Supreme Judicial Court, but every argument failed. On July 9, 1931, Belenski was finally sentenced to death. Daly made an appeal for clemency to Governor Joseph B. Ely, on the grounds that Belenski's confession was nonsensical and proved he was not mentally competent to have stood trial. Furthermore, after having been confined to prison, Belenski had been diagnosed with a case of mild epilepsy. The governor asked Daly whether there was any question that his client had murdered the Stefanowiczes. Daly said there was not but that the appeal for clemency was not based on innocence; rather, it was the state that had failed to prove that Belenski was sane. Ultimately, the governor declined to intervene.

Belenski spent his last few days in the death house at Charlestown State Prison smoking; in prayer with the prison chaplain, Reverend Ralph W.

Farrell; and receiving visits from his brother and his son and his daughter. Daly, the attorney who had spent over a year fighting for his life, chose to say goodbye to his illiterate client via a farewell letter. According to press accounts, shortly after midnight on October 20, 1931, Joseph Belenski entered the death chamber "with a blank expression on his face, glanced at the witnesses, turned and dropped into the electric chair," inscrutable until the end.

13

HUDSON, 1935

TORCH SLAYERS ALWAYS STUPID

Shortly before 10:30 p.m. on Monday, May 6, 1935, Merle Stratton looked down East Main Street in the direction of Sudbury and saw a flickering light. Realizing he was seeing flames, the forty-five-year-old mechanic ran back inside the filling station on the corner of Brook Street to notify Hudson's volunteer fire department. The firefighters rushed to the remote Lake Boon neighborhood, out past the poor farm. When they arrived, they found the wreck of a late-model sedan already burning out of control. It was too late to save whoever might be inside. The best they could do was make sure the fire did not spread any farther.

When the flames had died down, the charred remains of a man's body were discovered in the back seat. Hudson police sergeant John McPartland and patrolman Henry Fahey watched the firemen remove the body from the car. Both the man and the automobile's seat cushions had been doused with gasoline before ignition, but remarkably, not all of his coat had burned. He carried no identification, but there were a couple of singed pieces of paper in his pocket as well as two partially burned notebooks. State police trooper George Conn combed through the wreckage, finding a signet ring and set of keys that might also prove helpful in identifying the victim. Also found near his body was a crowbar.

The body might have been unrecognizable, but Massachusetts license plate number 661805 was still on the vehicle. State troopers called to the scene found one of the victim's shoes on the other side of the road. It looked to be of the type manufactured in state prisons. They also found a fresh set of tire tracks leading away from the site. State detectives Edward P. O'Neill and Edward J. Sherlock, who had investigated the Stow farmhouse murder five years earlier, were once again called to investigate, and they immediately started to make connections. The gangland-style execution prompted them to contact Rhode Island police investigating the Rettich mob, and when the car registration was traced to Revere, they wondered if it could be linked to two other recent murders there. But the place to begin was with a visit to the home of the car's owner, fifty-year-old candy maker Francesco "Frank" DiStasio. At 3:00 a.m. Tuesday morning, the two detectives knocked on the door of DiStasio's apartment in the two-family home at 64 Reservoir Avenue, Revere.

The door was answered by Frank's twenty-three-year-old son, Anthony, who shared the apartment with his wife, Shirley, and his father. His mother, Maria Giuseppina "Josephine" (Morandi) DiStasio, had died less than two months earlier, he explained. Anthony identified the ring as looking very much like one that his father wore. Furthermore, Frank DiStasio was now missing. The two had had plans to meet in East Boston at 1:00 p.m. the day before, but his father had never showed. The dead man was about the same age as Frank, wearing Frank's ring and found in Frank's car. Anthony, a dapper and good-looking young man with an air of earnestness about him, was eager to help the detectives solve the mystery of how his father had wound up in Hudson. O'Neill and Sherlock decided to take Anthony in for further questioning.

Anthony DiStasio had at first provided an alibi for his whereabouts between 6:30 and 11:30 p.m. on May 6, but it was easily refuted when his witnesses refused to vouch for him. Meanwhile, medical examiner Dr. Norman M. Hunter had had a chance to conduct an autopsy on the body found in Frank DiStasio's car. He found that the skull had been crushed, and both arms and both legs had been fractured. Despite the obvious trauma suffered by the victim, he had died from smoke inhalation after the automobile had been set ablaze. In the doctor's best judgment, the man had been about forty-five years old, five feet, seven inches tall, with a wiry build and brown hair. The investigators still did not know who the man was, but Dr. Hunter could tell them who it was not: Frank DiStasio. DiStasio was five feet, eleven inches tall, had gray hair on his temples and weighed two hundred pounds.

If the detectives had imagined they would find the young DiStasio an easy nut to crack, they were proven entirely correct. Without an alibi and confronted with the evidence that his father was not the body in the car, Anthony calmly began to tell the detectives what had happened on the evening of May 6, 1935. Not only did it take less than a day to put together the story of that fateful Monday night, but they were also able to brief local reporters in time for the story to make it into the bulldog editions of the Boston papers early Wednesday morning.

The plan had come together in the five weeks since the death of Anthony's mother on March 30. Newly widowed Frank DiStasio was deep in debt. Working in candy factories barely covered the bills in the best of times, and the mid-1930s were hardly the best of times. Richard J. DeNeil, the undertaker who had arranged for his late wife's burial, had put a lien on the cash surrender value of his life insurance policy until he was paid. Furthermore, DiStasio still owed $1,350 on his new car. After he had fallen behind on payments, it had been repossessed and was sitting in Sam Waugh's garage in Revere.

It was time for a fresh start. With his wife dead, Frank was free to marry his girlfriend, Ethel Reilly. Reilly, a matronly thirty-nine-year-old East Boston woman, had met Frank when they had worked together at a candy factory. But how could he support a new wife when he didn't even have the money to bury the old one?

On April 11, he filed paperwork with the Equitable Life Assurance Society of the United States to take out a $5,000 insurance policy on his life, making his son, Anthony, the beneficiary. Combined with his existing coverage, the total payout would be $20,400, a reasonable if hardly exorbitant sum in 1935. The policy was delivered on April 24. He somehow managed to come up with enough money to get his new car out of hock. Then on May 5, Frank took Ethel and his son out for a Sunday drive and picnic in the country—Lake Boon in Hudson.

At 7:00 p.m. the next day, Frank and Anthony met up in the South End of Boston. Frank was driving his old sedan while his son followed behind in the new car. On Union Park Street, Anthony saw his father pull up alongside a shabbily dressed man standing on the sidewalk. After a few minutes of conversation, the man climbed in beside the elder DiStasio, and the car pulled away. The two cars traveled in tandem for the thirty-mile drive to Lake Boon. On the Post Road in Sudbury, a tire on Frank's car blew out. If his passenger had not previously observed that another car was trailing them, he certainly noticed now, because Anthony pulled over to help his father change the flat. Soon afterward, the DiStasio caravan was back underway. Crossing the Hudson town line, Frank continued on ahead while Anthony pulled over. The son dutifully turned the car around and waited for his father. After about fifteen minutes, Frank got into the car, and the two headed back to Boston. Anthony dropped off his father and then drove to their Revere apartment.

Anthony emphasized that he had neither heard nor seen anything, never mind participated in the murder. Legally, these distinctions meant little, as he had acknowledged knowing about the plan beforehand and assisting his father in committing it. Because he had never spoken to the man, he could not even help the detectives identify the victim.

While Anthony did not volunteer the information to the police, the DiStasios had not planned on picking a stranger off the street to be their anonymous victim. Instead, one Fred Wagner of 13½ Howard Street, Boston, had originally been slated to play the role of the late Frank DiStasio. Frank had first met the intended victim in the early 1920s, when Wagner had worked as the bouncer at a speakeasy owned by one of Frank's relatives. According to the account he later told police, Fred Wagner had received a call from Anthony DiStasio on Friday night, May 3. Anthony told the unemployed Wagner that his father might have a job for him. He was to meet Frank at 8:00 a.m. Saturday morning in Brattle Square to discuss the opportunity. After Wagner expressed his sympathies for the recent death of Frank's wife, Josie, the two got down to business. The job was at a candy factory in Providence, Frank said. Wagner should meet him at a Washington Street tavern at 5:30 p.m. on Monday, May 6, and the two could drive to Rhode Island together. Wagner occasionally worked odd jobs for local market men, and on Monday, he was unable to leave until 5:45 p.m. By the time Wagner arrived at the bar, Frank had already given up and left. Wagner was so desperate for work that he tried to find out where he had gone, but nobody knew. After asking around, he found out that the DiStasios did not even have a telephone. One of the exasperated patrons scoffed at him, "Why are you so excited? Frank doesn't have a job for you!" Wagner's disappointment at missing a job opportunity turned to relief a few days later when he saw the newspapers. (Although Wagner fit the bill in that his sudden disappearance would have aroused little notice, he was considerably shorter and thinner than Frank DiStasio. It is unlikely that his body would have fooled the police, either.)

On Wednesday, May 8, the morning editions of the Boston papers contained Anthony's version of events in full, as well as a picture of the missing Frank DiStasio. Later that day, a sharp-eyed Boston police officer named William Dooley recognized Frank walking along Commonwealth Avenue and arrested him without incident. At first, Frank accused his son of lying and making up the whole story, but he eventually confirmed Anthony's account. The only difference was that he maintained his son had no knowledge of the murder beforehand, as Frank did not know that Anthony's own words and actions had already told the detectives otherwise.

Middlesex County district attorney Warren L. Bishop had the DiStasios promptly indicted for the murder of John Doe. The ambitious district attorney had held office for four years and in 1934 was reelected by the largest margin of any Republican officeholder in Massachusetts in a particularly Democratic year. The *Boston Globe* later characterized his tenure in office, perhaps somewhat euphemistically, as "lively." He thought of himself as a crusader and did not shy away from conflict with local police departments, town officials or anyone else for that matter. He had begun his political career as a progressive Democrat, serving in the state senate. A week before the election in 1919, he dramatically renounced his party to endorse Calvin Coolidge's reelection as governor because he refused "to be in partnership with Bolshevism and anarchy." (One supposes that this mystified the Democratic nominee for governor that year, Richard H. Long, who owned a shoe factory in Framingham and would soon found the Bay State automobile company.)

Bishop wanted a June trial, the perfect run-up to his announcement that he would be running for the GOP gubernatorial nomination in 1936. It was said to be the first instance in county history of an indictment for murder where the victim's identity was unknown. Since the victim's identity had nothing to do with the motive or circumstances of his demise, Bishop was confident in his case. Detectives declared it unlikely that they would ever learn who had died in Frank DiStasio's car, given that he was badly burned and probably lived on the margins of society.

But, as with everything else in this case, the answer came surprisingly quickly. One unburned page in the victim's notebook read, "April 13—2½ hours—Drumy; April 15—2½ hours—Clark; April 16—3½ hours— McCarthy." It was published in the newspapers, and Daniel J. Crowley of Dorchester immediately knew what the words meant. He worked in the freight yards of the Boston and Maine Railroad, and employees were required to keep a log of their hours worked and the foreman who supervised them, three of whom were named Drumy, Clark and McCarthy. Detectives checked employee logs at the yard and determined that the hours had been worked by one Daniel M. Crowley. (That both employees were named Daniel Crowley is a coincidence; they were completely unrelated.) Going to 105 Green Street in the West End, the address found on the pay record, the detectives interviewed his landlady. Agnes Labor said Daniel Crowley had been living there for eight months, but she hadn't seen him since 2:00 p.m. on Monday afternoon, when he headed out the door carrying two bundles. She added that he had been continually intoxicated for the previous week and was still in his cups when he left three days earlier. Sherlock and O'Neill had brought with them the blackened keys from the automobile and discovered one fit the door to the street, the second fit the door to Crowley's room and the third fit a suitcase they found inside. In the suitcase they found Crowley's passport, complete with photograph. Using the passport, the police were able to receive confirmation from both Frank DiStasio and workers at the B&M yard that this was the same man. Agnes Labor was able to identify the remains of the victim's clothing as those worn by Crowley on Monday.

So, who had Frank picked up that evening? By all accounts, Daniel M. Crowley drank heavily and had no visitors to his small room on the third floor at Mrs. Labor's house. He worked sporadically as an unskilled laborer. He had been born on March 5, 1882, in County Cork, Ireland, and immigrated to the United States in 1920, immediately swearing out citizenship papers. He had a cousin in Chicago and another back in Ireland, but no other kin could be identified. (As it happens, his murderer was also an immigrant. Frank DiStasio had been born in Italy on May 11, 1885, and had immigrated with his uncle to Boston's North End in about 1906. Anthony and his mother were both first-generation natural-born U.S. citizens.)

It seems unlikely that the DiStasios had access to newspapers from their cells in the Middlesex County Jail in East Cambridge, where they awaited trial for first-degree murder. Perhaps it was just as well, as the May 12 *Boston Sunday Globe* added insult to the DiStasios' (self-inflicted) injury with an article bearing the title "Torch Slayers Always Stupid." Reporter Padraic King noted that the conviction rate for insurance fraud where another body was substituted for the insured was roughly 100 percent. King failed to note that any successful torch murders would have gone undiscovered by definition and therefore would not show up in the statistics. Given the rapidity with which the DiStasios' criminal enterprise unraveled, they certainly were in no position to argue with King's central thesis.

On May 24, sixteen days after they were charged with a capital offense, the DiStasios met with an attorney. That they had an attorney at all was something of a novelty. For 142 years, the right of the accused "to have the assistance of counsel for his defense" guaranteed by the Sixth Amendment to the Constitution meant that if you had hired a lawyer, the court had to let him represent you. Anybody lacking the means to hire an attorney was on his own. With *Powell v. Alabama* (the "Scottsboro boys" case) in 1932, the

Supreme Court had ruled that defendants in death penalty cases had the right to effective counsel. So, Frank and Anthony had a court-appointed attorney to represent them, William Randolph "Billy" Scharton.

Scharton was probably the most renowned, if controversial, defense lawyer in Boston. His lifetime record in thirty-eight capital cases was thirty acquittals, six convictions for second-degree murder (and therefore spared the death penalty) and only two convictions. A native of Virginia, Scharton studied law at Yale and New York University (though he held a degree from neither). He came to settle in Boston at the turn of the century after returning from his service in the Spanish-American War. While waiting in court on a motor vehicle issue, he was told he was privileged to witness one of the finest members of the Boston bar argue the case immediately preceding his own. He decided then and there to practice in the Commonwealth, since he was certain he could do better. He attributed his success with juries to his ability to gain the sympathy of the "common man," and most of all, he never bored them. He ran afoul of the Internal Revenue Service in 1934 but successfully defended himself against tax fraud. During Prohibition, he also once famously told a federal agent that he had ten barrels of whisky at his Reading property, Patricia Farms, "and if you come down and take it, I'll shoot you full of holes." He was often chastised by judges for his aggressive courtroom demeanor, but he was also known for a brilliant mind and his mastery of the most arcane details of civil procedure and the law.

When he agreed to represent the DiStasios, Scharton was coming off of one of his few losses. His client, Massachusetts Institute of Technology graduate Abraham Faber, had been convicted in connection with the notorious Millen brothers' crime spree and was due to be executed on June 7, 1935. Looking back on his career, he characterized his death penalty defendants generally as an undistinguished and contemptible lot "because all but Abe Faber were dumb." (See James L. Parr's book *Dedham: Historic and Heroic Tales from Shiretown* for more information about the Faber case.)

After several delays, including one owing to Scharton's withdrawal as counsel for Frank DiStasio on the grounds that Anthony and Frank's interests were now divergent, the selection of the jurors began on October 28, 1935. Scharton immediately objected to the proceedings on the grounds that prosecutors and police already had interviewed many of the prospective jurors and sought permission to cross-examine them. Judge Nelson P. Brown ruled that while he certainly frowned on the practice, he would do all the questioning of the jurors and would not permit a "fishing expedition." The jury was selected, and the trial began the next day.

Over the course of a week, the prosecution methodically laid out the facts of the case. Scharton and Edward M. Shanley, who now represented Frank DiStasio, cross-examined the prosecution's witnesses. On November 7, Shanley took up Frank's defense. He argued that since Frank's wife's death, Frank had been on a "general debauch." He had never previously smoked or drank, but his mental state had become so impaired due to alcohol saturation that his mind was effectively a blank between April 6 and May 16, ten days after the alleged crime. His confession had solely been a father's attempt to save his son, Anthony, who was the true mastermind. Scharton declined to make any defense for Anthony. Instead, he filed a motion with Judge Brown for a directed verdict of not guilty, on the grounds that while Anthony had been placed at the scene of the murder, there had been no evidence presented that he had any foreknowledge of the crime and therefore could not be convicted of conspiracy to commit murder. Brown agreed, and on November 13, Anthony DiStasio was declared not guilty. Meanwhile, he would continue to be held as an accessory before the

Frank and Anthony DiStasio became the first father and son to both die in the electric chair at Charlestown State Prison. *Courtesy of the Boston Public Library, Leslie Jones Collection.*

fact. On November 14, 1935, after an hour and a half of deliberation, the jury handed down its verdict on Frank—guilty.

Despite Scharton's best efforts, Anthony DiStasio's reprieve was only temporary. Six months later, he was tried and convicted of being an accessory to the murder, a charge that also carried a mandatory death penalty. Scharton continued to make appeals on behalf of both Anthony and Frank, but all ultimately failed. After writing one last letter to his wife, Anthony DiStasio entered the execution chamber at 12:03 a.m. on January 17, 1938. Two minutes after his son was pronounced dead, Frank entered the chamber at 12:10. By 12:16, they had earned the distinction of being the first father and son in New England to have both died in the electric chair. Later that week, a crowd of fifteen thousand curiosity seekers filed past their bodies as they lay in an undertaker's parlor on Prince Street in Boston's North End, and St. Leonard's Church was filled to capacity for their funeral mass.

Ultimately, the legacy of that night near Lake Boon in May 1935 is one of profound loss. Daniel M. Crowley, Frank DiStasio and Anthony DiStasio lost their lives and Ethel Reilly her fiancé. William Scharton lost his second capital case. Despite his own wins in the courtroom, Warren Bishop lost his race for the Republican gubernatorial nomination in 1936. His "lively" style as district attorney had also lost him the support of the voters, who turned him out of office altogether in 1938.

In a fitting denouement, Shirley DiStasio, who had already lost her husband, lost his last letter to her. It was stolen out of her mailbox by a souvenir hunter before she even had a chance to read it.

14

SUDBURY, 1935

THE MURDER THAT WASN'T

In the summer of 1936, Seneca Wilson Hall had been a police officer in Sudbury for forty years, half of that time as chief. At age sixty-one, eleven years after breaking up the Klan riot (see chapter 10), "Sen" had no intention of retiring, but the town thought it was an occasion worth celebrating, nonetheless. On the evening of July 22, the entire population of nearly 1,200 was invited to an outdoor banquet held in his honor. Afterward, the Federal Theatre Project of the Works Progress Administration sponsored a free vaudeville show and dance at the town hall. Harvey Fairbank, chairman of the selectmen, acted as the master of ceremonies. Among the artists on the bill that night were La Verne & Ward, a boy and girl song and dance act; Marjorie Vettle, rag picture artist; Capt. Day & Brown, light comedy; and Vangard, Cape & Vangard, "a musical turn."

Sen Hall used the event to reflect on the changes in police work since he had started as a part-timer in 1896. In those days, "practically all there was to do was to take care of drunks and watch for chicken thieves." Most of Sudbury lacked telephone service, so if somebody needed him, they had to find him at his parents' farm or stop him on his early-morning milk route. (Even in 1936, Hall still began his day delivering milk.) With the coming of the automobile, it became necessary to institute regular patrols, and on Sundays, he engaged the services of two uniformed men to help direct traffic. Hall embraced the coming of technology. His patrol car was equipped with a wireless, so it was only necessary to telephone his wife, Marion, at his home. She would then relay the message to the state police barracks in Framingham, who could contact him by radio wherever he was in the town.

Still, most of his work required defusing a quarrel before it became a feud and making sure teenage mischief did not become a steppingstone to criminal activity. The holiday camps on the ponds in Sudbury were a source of trouble, often used as hideouts for fugitives from Boston during the off-season. "Recently at one of those camps, I arrested a man with a holdup record," Hall recalled. "He had been stealing turkeys."

But in forty years, he had never had to handle a murder. "At least anything that turned out to be a murder," he allowed. His listeners did not have to be reminded of the peculiar events that had taken place at an isolated cottage on Hudson Road eight months earlier.

The cottage was the home of forty-seven-year-old Charles W. Hamilton, his forty-five-year-old wife, Rachel J. "Jennie" Hamilton, and their eleven-year-old daughter Helen. Charles had previously worked as a stripper for Cambridge printer J. Frank Facey until 1934. He moved to Sudbury once he had found a job as a laborer working on the construction of the Concord Turnpike. It was hardly ideal—for example neither of the Hamiltons knew how to drive, having lived all their lives in the city—but it was a job, and jobs were hard to find six years into the Great Depression. But with the end of the good weather, the job ended, too, and he found himself unemployed again.

So, he must have welcomed the opportunity to host his friend Forest L. Stetson for a week at the end of October 1935. Stetson was a thirty-five-year-old store clerk on Nantucket, where he had grown up. His father was a carpenter, and Forest had dropped out of school after eighth grade to help support the family. He mostly worked as a store clerk, but he had spent time several years earlier working as a laborer for mason George Folger. He fell in love with Folger's daughter Inez, twelve years his junior, and they were married on September 23, 1934. Though practically still newlyweds, they had already seen tough times. Inez had suffered two nervous breakdowns in her life, and two months after their wedding, she had tried to commit suicide by walking out into Nantucket Harbor. Now, a year later, they were enjoying Forest's two-week vacation.

After a week in Boston, the Stetsons spent a week with the Hamiltons out in the country. On several days, they were joined by Forest's seventeen-year-old nephew, Herbert Stetson, who worked for automobile mechanic Stephen Clouther in Allston. Clouther and Hamilton had struck a deal: Hamilton bought a car that Clouther could use as long as he came to Sudbury regularly to drive them. One of the activities they all enjoyed was target shooting with Herbert Stetson's .22-caliber rifle, which he left in the hallway at the Hamiltons' cottage, along with a box of cartridges placed on the nearby stairs. When it came time for Forest to return to work in Nantucket, Inez decided to stay in Sudbury for another week.

That Friday, November 8, 1935, Inez sat down to lunch with Charles and Jennie Hamilton at 1:30 p.m. (Helen was at school.) Afterward, the women washed dishes in the kitchen while Charles went to the parlor for a cigarette and a lie down on the couch. As Jennie finished the drying, Inez went into the hall, picked up Herbert's gun and playfully pointed it through the doorway at Charles on the couch six feet away. A moment later, Inez Stetson discharged the rifle into Charles Hamilton's groin.

"Jennie come here, I've shot Charles!" shouted Inez. "What's that?" the older woman replied, before entering the room and seeing her husband bleeding and unconscious on the sofa. "Where do I get a doctor?" Jennie sent Inez across the road to the neighbors while she ran into the kitchen for a glass of water. She poured it over her husband's head while she cradled him, and Charles revived long enough to say, "Don't cry; I will be all right." After another moment, he mumbled softly, "Don't let Inez worry because she couldn't help it."

Outside Inez ran across the road screaming, "Get a doctor! I've shot a man!" Hearing her, Mrs. Austin Horne ran down the road to the Goodnow place, where she telephoned for Chief Hall. On the way back, Horne flagged down a passing automobile, and they proceeded to carry Hamilton, in great pain and crying out, from the house and into the car. Jennie and Inez accompanied Charles on the ride to Emerson Hospital in Concord, but he died from massive bleeding shortly after arrival. On hearing the news, Inez fainted.

Chief Hall was joined in the questioning of Inez and Jennie at the Concord State Police barracks by Lieutenant Edward J. Sherlock and Lieutenant Edward P. O'Neill. All quickly agreed that Inez Stetson held no animosity toward the victim and that she had not intended to kill Charles Hamilton. There were some nagging questions, however.

Stephen Clouther had been the last person to use the rifle the day before the incident. He adamantly insisted that he could not have possibly left the one-shot gun loaded after target shooting. Inez also denied having loaded (or cocked) the gun, but she had left the kitchen about a minute before Jennie had heard the shot, leaving Inez plenty of time to insert a cartridge. A long-distance phone call placed to husband Forest Stetson in Nantucket revealed her previous breakdowns and her attempted suicide the year before. Had her shooting of Hamilton resulted from a similar impulse? They decided to hold her overnight in Framingham and requested that she be sent to

Westborough State Hospital for observation. As she was being led from the Concord barracks to the car that would take her to Framingham, Inez laughed and joked with the reporters she encountered waiting outside.

Saturday morning, November 9, 1935, Inez Stetson was examined by eminent Framingham psychiatrist Dr. Solomon Carter Fuller and his colleague Dr. F.C. Southworth, who recommended she should be held for observation. After Framingham district court judge Edward W. Blodgett signed the thirty-five-day commitment papers, Chief Hall and state police sergeant Michael J. Noonan drove her to Westborough. When the thirty-five days were up on December 13, she was released; Dr. Walter E. Lang had found her competent. Since she had not been charged with any crime, Inez returned to Nantucket and her ailing husband Forest, who was hospitalized with appendicitis.

Less than a week later, Inez was back in police custody. On December 18, the judge presiding over an inquest ruled that while she had not acted deliberately, nonetheless she had shown "reckless and wanton disregard of the life and safety of Charles Hamilton." The Middlesex district attorney, Warren L. Bishop, immediately obtained a warrant for her arrest for manslaughter. She cooperated with the Nantucket police, who placed her on a steamer for New Bedford, where she was again met by the erstwhile Chief Hall and a state trooper. New York State chief judge Sol Wachtler once famously observed that a district attorney could get a grand jury to indict a ham sandwich. Nevertheless, on January 10, 1936, district attorney Bishop failed to get a Middlesex County grand jury to indict Inez Stetson for manslaughter, and she was freed the next day.

Seneca Hall remained Sudbury's police chief until his career was derailed by a controversy over another accidental death five years later. On February 18, 1940, North Sudbury resident Johnny Kalilanen was run over and killed by a town snowplow. Chief Hall investigated the accident and determined that the plow driver had been responsible, which put the town in a poor position since it carried no liability insurance. The selectmen dismissed Hall on December 11, 1941, listing a number of grievances, with the board secretary further noting that "his conduct of matters involving possible liability to the town was not in the town's best interests." Chief Hall passed away in 1957.

Meanwhile, Inez returned to Nantucket, where she seems to have lived a long, quiet life. Perhaps unsurprisingly, her marriage to Forest Stetson had ended in divorce by 1940. But she married a second time and got a job working in the kitchen at the Nantucket Cottage Hospital. She died on September 28, 2003, at the age of ninety-one, taking with her the secret of what had really happened that Friday afternoon at the Hamilton cottage in 1935.

15

SAXONVILLE, 1959

DEATH IN SUBURBIA

America of the 1950s has acquired a certain nostalgic glow over the ensuing decades. It was the childhood years of the baby boomers, the largest generation. Even those born too late to remember the 1950s saw the years in idealized form on television through repeats of *Father Knows Best* or *Leave It to Beaver*. As early as the 1970s, the comedy *Happy Days* celebrated a seemingly simpler time when the United States was the world's most prosperous nation and the undisputed leader of the free world. Reality, of course, was always more complicated.

For Ella Monaco, a forty-two-year-old housecleaner in Framingham's Saxonville neighborhood, the 1950s were hardly a golden age. But she had never had an easy time of it. On Tuesday, August 18, 1959, as she sat in the modern kitchen of 25 Bradford Road, she lamented her lifetime of "bad luck" to her employer, Sherrill (Glovsky) Schiff. The Schiffs had moved into their brand-new ranch house in the Pinefield development the year before, just in time for the birth of their first son, Daniel. (Their second son, Adam, as of this writing a congressman from California who served as the lead manager of the first impeachment of President Donald Trump, would be born in 1960.) The Schiffs were the kind of young family that was moving from Boston to the suburbs. Sherrill was twenty-six, and her thirty-one-year-old husband, Edward, was a salesman for a New York company. In 1966, they would move to a larger home in Framingham, before moving west in 1969.

Although Ella Monaco lived less than a mile from the Schiffs' home, in a sense, she lived in a whole different world. She was born in 1917, the tenth child of Clifford and Etta Sherman of Westfield, Massachusetts. Clifford worked as a patternmaker in a foundry, but he became ill and lost his job. Etta had to go to work, so she boarded out six-week-old Ella to a neighboring family. When Etta found herself unable to pay her daughter's board, that family adopted her. (In fact, the entire Sherman family was dispersed. In the 1920 census, Clifford and Etta were both working as attendants at the Monson State Hospital and lived on the premises, but none of their children were living with them.)

About 1926, when Ella was nine, according to Ella's sister, Olive, "something happened to that family" that had adopted her. Ella became a ward of the commonwealth, which placed her in a residential school. After she turned eighteen, she was boarded out to a family in Maynard. A few years later, she studied to be an attendant nurse at Medfield State Hospital. She had two children in the early 1950s—Paul, born in July 1951, and Tommy, born in October 1953. It is unclear from the records whether she was married or who the father was. In 1954, however, she married Richard Frederick "Dick" Monaco. He was twenty years old, and she was thirty-seven. Dick's father, Domenico Antonio Monaco, was a native of Pietranico, Italy, who had immigrated to the United States in 1910 and found work as a gardener on a private estate in Weston. According to Ella's sister, Dick had been in a car crash at the age of fourteen that resulted in his being hospitalized for three years. He still suffered the effects from the accident years later, "so his work wasn't too steady." It fell to Ella to work extra hard to support her children.

Ella Monaco had woken up early that sweltering Tuesday. It was humid and would be the fourth straight day where the temperature would hit the nineties. She wasn't due to clean the Schiffs' house until 9:00 a.m., but she had told Mrs. Schiff that she would be there early to get as much done as possible before the worst of the heat hit. The Monacos' second-floor apartment at 3 Park Avenue was a far cry from the Schiffs' open-plan ranch house. The old Victorian house was split into four apartments in a neighborhood dominated by the Roxbury Carpet factory. Ella roused her son Paul and husband, Dick, who had gotten home at about midnight from his job working as a dishwasher and cook at the Piety Corner Diner in Waltham. They piled into their newly acquired two-door light green 1953 Ford and drove the short distance to Mechanic Street, where Ella hopped out to pay their twelve-dollar weekly rent. Knocking at Magdalena (Cselinszki) Welch's door at 7:30 a.m., she only stayed long enough to hand over the money. Dick then drove up to the Schiffs' house on Bradford Road and dropped her off.

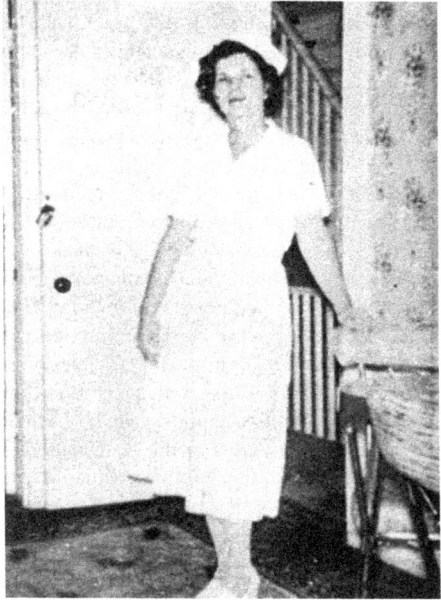

Ella Monaco in her nurse's uniform. *Courtesy of Framingham History Center.*

At about 11 a.m., Ella had mentioned she hadn't had time to have breakfast that morning, so Sherrill Schiff got her an early lunch. Mrs. Schiff admitted she hadn't spoken much to Ella until that day. Ella had only been cleaning houses for a few weeks. Before that, she worked as a nurse at the Hanson Nursing Home in South Natick. But when Paul was out riding his bike and got hit by a car early in the summer, Ella quit her job so that she could have him with her. While they shared lunch, Ella told Sherrill about her life of bad luck. She shared that her younger son, Tommy, had fallen out of his crib at the age of two and a half while she had been at work. He was brought to the hospital but died from a blood clot. It was right afterward that she had moved to Saxonville. She had friends who told her, "I'm staying away from you, Ella, you're bad luck." Sherrill tried to buoy the older woman's spirits, saying, "Maybe that's all past now, Ella. Maybe you'll have good luck from now on." After lunch, Dick dropped Paul off on his way to work at the diner. Paul went across the street to 20 Bradford Road to play with his friend, Allan Carlson. He popped back over to get a dime from his mother for ice cream. Ella gave him two dimes to make sure Allan also got an ice cream. At about

4:00 p.m., she finished up work and walked to Carl and Julia Carlsons' to pick up Paul. The Carlsons invited Paul to stay over for dinner and a swim in their pool, so Ella said to be sure her son left by 7:30 p.m. After a short detour back to the Schiffs' to retrieve the ball Paul had left out on their lawn, she walked back to her apartment.

At 6:30 p.m., one of her neighbors at 3 Park Avenue saw her sipping iced coffee out in the yard. She had changed out of her housedress. At 8:30 p.m., with still no sign of Paul, Ella set out down the slope behind the house to the Pinefield Shopping Plaza below. Barbara Cowland, another tenant at 3 Park Avenue, saw her head down to the plaza's parking lot. There she spoke to a man and then turned north on Nicholas Road in the direction of Bradford Road. That was the last confirmed sighting anyone had of Ella Monaco.

Mrs. Carlson had indeed sent Paul on his way at 7:30 p.m., at the conclusion of the syndicated television show *Waterfront*, a drama about a Los Angeles tugboat captain that had already been in reruns for several years. But Paul stopped at the Rodriguez house at 84 Nicholas Road, just on the far side of the Hultman aqueduct, less than half a mile from the Monaco apartment. Paul returned home a short time later, but his mother had already left. The eight-year-old waited patiently outside on the steps for her to return and then went inside, where Dick Monaco found him after returning home from work at about 12:30 a.m. After talking to Paul, Dick notified the Framingham Police that his wife was missing at 12:52 a.m. and then called again Wednesday morning. In the afternoon, he called the state police. When there was still no sign of her on Thursday, Monaco made a personal appeal over the local AM radio station, WKOX, for anyone who had information to contact the authorities.

Ella Monaco walked down this path leading from her apartment house down to Nicholas Road on the evening she was murdered. *Courtesy of Framingham History Center.*

age as Paul Monaco, and lived with his parents at 353 Water Str
was accompanied by ten-year-old Judy Healey, who lived at 307
Street, and her German Shepherd, Ringer, who was the star of
game as Rin Tin Tin. As they stopped to throw pebbles into a
Ringer began rooting around in the undergrowth. When the c
went to see what the dog had found, they saw "a woman sleepi
blood on her." Running back to the Swanson home, they insisted th
found a real woman and not a discarded mannequin. Mrs. Swan
skeptical but nonetheless called Framingham police. Patrolman T.
Wlodyka, who coincidentally also lived on Park Avenue just ac
street from the Monacos, was sent to look into the report. The c
led him to the body, just beyond the brook thirty feet below wha
84 Joseph Road, in the scrub growth past a shelf of debris that ha
dumped down into the ravine when the road was laid out. Though
facedown and he did not want to move the body until it could be p
documented, Wlodyka tentatively identified her from her clothin
missing neighbor, Ella Monaco.

It might not have helped even if Patrolman Wlodyka had seen h
She was beaten about the head so severely that her face was unrecog
Dr. J. Harry McCann, the Framingham medical examiner, determi
had died from blunt force trauma. She suffered a dozen knife cuts,
none deep enough to be fatal, and a *V* was carved into her chest,
after her death. The reed grass for about ten feet around had been fl
indicating a prolonged struggle. There were bloodstained rocks
ground to either side of her head that had probably been the weapo
against her. Police theorized that she had been attacked with a knife,
the penknife found under her body, although maybe a larger blade
feet, ten inches and 145 pounds, she had been strong enough to
this initial attack but then was beaten to death by her attacker, v
wielding rocks. She still had on her nurse's shoes, white blouse and
her Bermuda shorts and panties had been cut from her body and wer
a short distance away. She had not been raped, however.

Dr. McCann, assisted by Harvard University pathologist Dr.
Katsas, performed a full autopsy at the Cookson Funeral Home or
Avenue in Framingham, which confirmed McCann's initial findin
Monaco was brought by police to identify the body but was so sha

Top: Ella Monaco's body was found in the trees down a ravine in a yet-to-be-built section of the Pinefield subdivision. The location of Joseph Road at the top of the slope is indicated by the telephone poles. *Courtesy of Framingham History Center*.

Bottom: Framingham police chief Edward T. McCarthy (*leaning over*) next to a priest as he administers last rites for Ella Monaco, August 20, 1959. *Courtesy of Framingham History Center.*

the body so disfigured that he found he could not. Her identity was later confirmed by examining her dental records, although a number of her teeth had been broken during the vicious assault.

After viewing the body, Framingham police chief Edward T. McCarthy spoke to reporters. He had joined the force in 1924 and been promoted to sergeant in 1937 and chief in January 1946. During that time, he had seen a lot of change in the town, including its population more than doubling from under twenty thousand in 1924 to well over forty thousand by 1959. "We obviously have the most fiendish sex pervert on the loose that has ever been seen in this area. This is one of the most horrible murders that I have seen in my 30 years as a police officer. We will get this fiend…and we will shoot to kill."

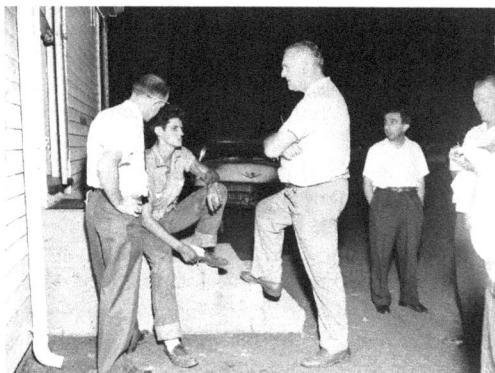

Chief McCarthy (*standing with foot on step*) talking to Dick Monaco (*seated*) outside the Monaco apartment on the night Ella's body was found. *Courtesy of Framingham History Center.*

Over the next several days, two neighbors came forward to admit that they might have seen or heard something. Lowell W. Lowell, who lived at 365 Water Street, not far from where Monaco's body was found, came forward first. He was out in the backyard cutting grass. "It was a hot night, and I had a cold drink out there. I was going in to get a second, when I heard a woman's voice, some distance away. She was saying 'no, no, no.'" Lowell then went inside to grab a flashlight, only to find the batteries were dead. After rooting around for replacements, he went outside again after maybe ten minutes. He heard a noise he described as "snarling," and then all was silent. "In my mind I was thinking, 'my wife and daughter are down the Cape, vacationing, so they are all right.'"

Herbert R. Nachtrab Jr. lived farther up Joseph Road. He had been out playing golf at the Sandy Burr Country Club in Wayland on that Tuesday. At dusk, he suddenly remembered it was his wife's birthday and they were supposed to go out that evening. He rushed home. As he rounded the curve on Joseph Road, "My headlights picked up a strange sight. There are some bushes there on that ledge of gravel. I saw a woman's legs, and white shorts. She seemed to be standing in the bushes, and there was a face. I only had a glance, but I got the impression the head didn't belong with the legs...like it was someone else's head. My thought was it's a man's face...dark-haired and with big eyes." Fearing his wife's wrath, Nachtrab figured he had caught two teenagers in the bushes and thought nothing more of it until Monaco's body was found at that spot two days later.

The investigation was led by Framingham police chief McCarthy, state police lieutenant detective Cornelius J. Crowley and Middlesex County assistant district attorney John Powers. They focused first on known sex offenders, roughly two hundred of whom were known to live in the surrounding communities. They were hauled in one by one and questioned. Other leads were followed, including a thirteen-year-old Natick girl who was accosted by a man in a vehicle with an indecent proposal the same night that Monaco was killed. A few days later, a twenty-seven-year-old Northborough man had tried to entice four young girls into his vehicle at Framingham's Lake Waushakum and then was spotted later and arrested at another town beach on Learned's Pond. As each lead was followed up, authorities continued to predict an early break to the case. On the day Ella Monaco was laid to rest in Mount Feake Cemetery in Waltham, exactly one week after she had disappeared, a police spokesman remarked, "I will tell you one thing: We're not working in the dark any longer."

But none of these leads seemed to pan out. (Perhaps unsurprisingly, as child sex predators were unlikely to have attacked the five-foot-ten and strong Ella Monaco.) Investigators theorized that after being seen walking north on Nicholas Road, Ella must have encountered someone she knew in an automobile and willingly gotten in. She was then driven to the site where her body was found and was killed after a struggle. Ella's son Paul was soon questioned, hoping he might reveal something, possibly about his stepfather. The husband is always the first suspect in a woman's murder, and Teresa Page, Ella's employer at the nursing home, did state that on occasion Ella had reported to work looking bruised. She never said who had hit her, however, and Ella had disappeared several hours before Dick Monaco returned from working at the diner. Friends agreed that she never would have abandoned her son for that long. Still, the time of death could have been after Dick had gotten off work, so after Ella's funeral, he was hauled into state police headquarters and questioned into the night. The next day, he returned, looking haggard and disheveled, to undergo a lie detector test. State police reported that he had passed and had in fact been cooperative with their inquiries all along. An obviously distraught Monaco spoke to reporters, saying, "I hope they find that killer. I'm not very good at talking and broadcasting. I loved my wife with all my heart. I pray the police catch him real quick."

At the instigation of Dick Monaco, police turned their attention to twenty-seven-year-old Walter Borisenko. Borisenko and his wife, Anna, were both friends of the Monacos and lived nearby on Centennial Place in Saxonville. Borisenko had been born in Poland on May 22, 1933, but both of his parents were killed during World War II. As a child, he had resettled in

Chief McCarthy ready to drive Dick Monaco to the station house for questioning. *Courtesy of Framingham History Center.*

the United States as a refugee. The Borisenkos had one child, Walter Jr., but all was not well. Borisenko was estranged from his wife and was on probation for having assaulted her in January. Dick Monaco had grown suspicious of the Polish immigrant's attentions to Ella. Police brought Borisenko in for questioning on Tuesday, September 1, 1959, exactly two weeks after Ella had disappeared.

In a dramatic turn of events, Middlesex County district attorney James L. O'Dea Jr. supervised the interrogation of Borisenko himself. It was unusual that O'Dea had heretofore left such a high-profile case to his assistant DA, John Powers, but he had been on vacation for almost the entire month of August. His unexpectedly long absence had prompted speculation in the press about where he had gone, but O'Dea had always kept his own counsel.

O'Dea had served as a marine in World War II, earning a Bronze Star and a Purple Heart during the Battle of Iwo Jima. After the war, he had gotten a Harvard Law degree and entered politics, first getting elected to the legislature from Lowell. Then he had pulled off a surprising upset in the 1956 election when he became the first Democrat to win the position of district attorney in Middlesex County in more than thirty years. (His victory was even more impressive given that Republican President Eisenhower easily carried Massachusetts that year with 60 percent of the vote in a romp over Adlai Stevenson.) O'Dea had been easily reelected in 1958, but now, speaking to the press before the Borisenko interrogation, the thirty-nine-year-old indicated he was contemplating retirement. When questioned about his whereabouts, he replied simply that he had been traveling in the Midwest and West, not Florida as had been reported, and that he was considering going into private practice.

The authorities questioned Borisenko for seven straight hours, releasing him at 12:30 a.m. Oddly, Borisenko did not simply go home. Instead, he went to see his wife, who was staying with her parents during their separation. He threw pebbles at her window until she woke up. The next day, Anna Borisenko told the police that he had said, "You think I killed Ella Monaco—well, I didn't." She refused to speak to him, however, and after a while, he left. She went on to say that she had only married him because he had threatened to kill himself otherwise. She left him after their arguments had grown violent, and he had threatened her with a knife.

The next morning, Walter Borisenko went to his construction job in Sudbury but that evening was taken in for more questioning. On Thursday, September 3, he willingly took a polygraph test administered by state police sergeant Walter Bogdanchik, who could speak Polish. Borisenko admitted to owning the penknife found beneath Monaco's body (although he claimed to have lost it months earlier) and to having spoken with her in the Pinefield Shopping Plaza parking lot the night she died. He claimed the bloodstains in his car were from a friend who had gone "picking" at the Wayland dump with him. (The friend corroborated this account.) As for Ella, Borisenko had wanted her to testify on his behalf in the divorce proceedings his wife had instigated against him, so he had a vested interest in her staying alive. The suspect's answers were so halting and disjointed, however, that it was determined the test was inconclusive. (A second polygraph exam on Saturday would also prove inconclusive due to Borisenko's state of nervous exhaustion.)

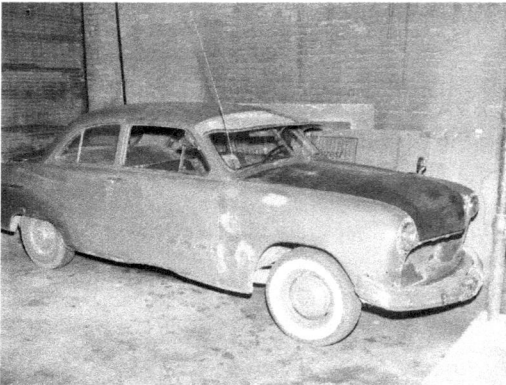

Walter Borisenko's car, in which a police forensics team discovered suspicious bloodstains. *Courtesy of Framingham History Center.*

On Friday, mounting tensions between police and prosecutors over the stalled investigation burst into public view. Captain Joseph Crescio, head of the state police detective unit, was briefing the press about the finding of bloodstains in Borisenko's automobile when Assistant District Attorney John Powers cut him off. "The district attorney's office assumed the responsibility for the investigation as soon as we were called in by Framingham police. *We* will give out all information that is to be released to the public." Crescio responded that the Monaco case was "a job that was botched from the start. As far as I know, the district attorney usually enters a case at the outset, determines the facts necessary for prosecution and then allows the *experienced* investigators to take over. He comes back into the case after the arrest to prosecute and take all the glory."

Over the next several days, the police reexamined Borisenko, who ultimately underwent six interrogations and three polygraph tests. Despite Framingham police chief McCarthy's statement on September 9 that an arrest was near, none came. On September 14, District Attorney O'Dea resigned to begin a new life in San Francisco, where he was hired by noted attorney Melvin Belli's firm. The reason for his mysterious disappearance in August became clear when he filed for divorce in Nevada later in the month. Not only had he been interviewing for jobs, but he had also established a residence in Reno.

Coincidentally, state police flew to Nevada a month later, but to Las Vegas, not Reno. There they interviewed twenty-two-year-old Charles Malcolm "Buddy" Gilmore. Even at that young age, Gilmore had already lived an eventful life. Originally from Natick, he went AWOL from the navy after enlisting at sixteen and was sent to the Kansas State Industrial Reformatory in Hutchinson, Kansas, at seventeen and a federal reformatory for interstate transportation of a stolen car after that. When he turned twenty-one, he was transferred to federal prison in Pennsylvania and then paroled in November 1958. He made his way to Saxonville and took up with an old girlfriend, Dorothy Ann Holmes, twenty, who had married Leslie Holmes in the interim. In October 1959, Buddy, Dorothy and her two children, aged four and ten months, were all found sleeping in a stolen car in Vegas. Las Vegas police discovered Buddy was wanted in connection with the Monaco investigation and alerted Massachusetts authorities. The Bay State detectives were unable to tie Gilmore to the murder, however, so they flew home empty-handed. (Buddy Gilmore died in California in 2018.)

Over the next several months, Ella's case would hit the papers again whenever police interviewed another potential suspect, but none warranted

The house where the Monacos lived in an apartment on the second floor, 2020. *Photo by author.*

a second mention. Soon years passed between mentions of the case, usually when a similar crime was committed elsewhere in New England or on the anniversary of Ella Monaco's death. Before the first anniversary, Walter Borisenko was involuntarily committed to the Westborough State Hospital by his former wife in early 1960, but he was released by 1963, when he obtained his U.S. citizenship and resided in Marlborough. He died in 1995 in a house fire in Cochituate started by a lit cigarette. Before the second anniversary, Framingham police chief Edward McCarthy died of a stroke in 1961, aged only sixty years old.

The case has never been solved. The last time the case received substantial attention in the press was over fifty years ago, on the tenth anniversary of the crime, in 1969. Dick Monaco later moved to Maine, where he remarried. He died at the age of seventy-eight in 2013, never knowing who had murdered his first wife. At this late date, it seems unlikely that we, too, will ever find out what happened to Ella Monaco on that sweltering August evening in 1959.

INDEX

ABOUT THE AUTHORS

Kevin A. Swope lives with his son in Framingham and works as a researcher for Babson College. He is the past president of the Framingham History Center, a member of the city's Historical Commission and author of *The Saxonville Mills: Three Centuries of Industry*, published by Damianos Publishing, and co-author with James L. Parr of *Framingham Legends and Lore*, published by The History Press.

James L. Parr lives in Framingham, where he has taught elementary school for over twenty-five years. He is the author of three poetry collections: *My Name Is James* and *Lost and Found*, both published by Damianos Publishing, and *Milestones*, a collection of poems inspired by Framingham history and published by the Framingham History Center. He is also the author of *Dedham: Historic and Heroic Tales of Shiretown* and co-author with Kevin A. Swope of *Framingham Legends and Lore*, both published by The History Press.

Find us on Facebook: Murder & Mayhem in Metrowest Boston.

www.ingramcontent.com/pod-product-compliance
Lightning Source LLC
Chambersburg PA
CBHW070335100426
42812CB00005B/1338